# Passing the
# Life in the UK Test

# Passing the Life in the UK Test

Megan Gibbins
Edited by Chris Taylor

In association with

Published by Learning Matters
33 Southernhay East
Exeter
EX1 1NX
info@learningmatters.co.uk
www.learningmatters.co.uk

British Cataloguing-in-Publication Data
A catalogue record for this book is available from the British Library.

ISBN 9781844452903

Cover design by Toucan Design
Text design by Phil Barker
Project Management by Diana Chambers
Typeset by Kelly Gray
Printed and bound in Great Britain by TJ International Ltd, Padstow, Cornwall

FSC
Mixed Sources
Product group from well-managed
forests and other controlled sources
Cert no. SGS-COC-2482
www.fsc.org
© 1996 Forest Stewardship Council

# Contents

**Introduction**     **1**

**Chapter 1   About this guide**     **3**
Section 1   The structure of this guide     3
Section 2   Who should take the test?     6
Section 3   Assessment activity     7
Section 4   Taking the test     13
Section 5   Study tips     15

**Chapter 2   A changing society**     **22**
Section 1   Migration to Britain     23
Section 2   The changing role of women     28
Section 3   Children, family and young people     32
Section 4   Revision questions and end of chapter checklist     41

**Chapter 3   The United Kingdom today: a profile**     **44**
Section 1   Population     46
Section 2   The nations and regions of the UK     52
Section 3   Religion     55
Section 4   Customs and traditions     59
Section 5   Revision questions and end of chapter checklist     64

**Chapter 4   How the United Kingdom is governed**     **67**
Section 1   The British Constitution     67
Section 2   The UK in Europe and the world     91
Section 3   Revision questions and end of chapter checklist     97

**Chapter 5   Everyday needs**     **101**
Section 1   Housing     102
Section 2   Services in and for the home     108
Section 3   Money and credit     114
Section 4   Health     120
Section 5   Education     129
Section 6   Leisure     138

Section 7  Travel and transport                                          142
Section 8  Revision questions and end of chapter checklist               149

**Chapter 6  Employment**                                               **153**
Section 1  Looking for work                                              154
Section 2  Equal rights and discrimination                              160
Section 3  At work                                                       163
Section 4  Working for yourself                                          172
Section 5  Childcare and children at work                               174
Section 6  Revision questions and end of chapter checklist               177

**Chapter 7  Glossary**                                                 **181**

**Chapter 8  Taking the test**                                          **203**
Section 1  Booking the test                                             204
Section 2  What to expect on the day of the test                        206
Section 3  Tips to help you when you take the test                      209
Section 4  What happens after the test?                                 211

**Practice tests**                                                      **212**

**Answers to practice tests**                                           **237**

**Answers to revision questions**                                       **241**

**Resources, references and useful websites**                           **244**

# Introduction

Congratulations! You have decided to make the commitment to become a British citizen and to take the *Life in the UK* test. The fact that you are reading this study guide shows that you are serious about passing the test. To help you, this complete self-study guide contains all the information that you need to feel prepared and confident when you take the test.

To save you money this guide includes all the official study material you will be tested on. It will take you through the process of passing the test in easy stages with hints and tips along the way.

The *Life in the UK* test was introduced by the government in 2005 and updated in 2007. One of the aims of the test is to give you information about the culture, traditions and way of life in Britain, and to prepare you to live in the country permanently.

To pass the test you will need to show that you have knowledge of life in the United Kingdom and that you have reached a certain level in your English language skills.

The questions in the test are not designed to catch you out, but to make sure you have read the study material in Chapters 2–6 of the official Home Office handbook, *Life in the United Kingdom: A Journey to Citizenship*. These are the chapters you will be tested on and these chapters are included, in full, in this guide.

This self-study guide will improve your chances of passing the test the first time.

It has been written clearly and concisely by experts in the field of Citizenship and English for speakers of other languages (ESOL).

**Figure I.1**   New citizens with Princess Anne at a citizenship ceremony.

# CHAPTER 1

# About this guide

This chapter will give you general information about the structure of this study guide and how you can get the most from it. There is information about who needs to take the test and how to apply for it. There is also an important section on study tips that will help you to prepare for the test.

The chapter is divided into the following five sections.

**Section 1** The structure of this guide.

**Section 2** Who should take the test?

**Section 3** Assessment activity.

**Section 4** Taking the test.

**Section 5** Study tips.

## SECTION 1 The structure of this guide

### How is this study guide organised?

In this guide the study material is presented in small manageable sections. To support the study material and to make it easier for you to remember, there are various tips and features. The features include: diagrams and summaries of the study material, *Helping you learn* tasks to check your progress and *Study tips*. There are also revision questions at the end of each chapter.

The most important section to read is the study material. You will need to read all of it to pass the test. As you go through the chapters you will see that there is a lot of information to remember. Completing the *Helping you learn* features, reading the *Study tips* and answering the revision questions will greatly improve your chances of passing the test first time.

In addition to the *Study tips* throughout the chapters, there is a more detailed section on general study tips at the end of Chapter 1. It is important to look at this section as you may learn some new tips that will help you.

The study material is presented in five easy to learn chapters. The five chapters are:

■ Chapter 2  A changing society;

■ Chapter 3  The United Kingdom today: a profile;

■ Chapter 4  How the United Kingdom is governed;

■ Chapter 5  Everyday needs;

■ Chapter 6  Employment.

Chapter 7 provides a glossary. This is a list of words and phrases from the study material that you may find difficult to understand. The list includes simple definitions and explanations to help you understand the words and phrases in the context in which they are used.

Chapter 8 provides detailed information about taking the test and what to expect on the day of the test.

At the back of the book, four practice tests are included to help you prepare for the test and to check that you are ready to take it.

The practice tests follow the same format as the *Life in the UK* test. As in the official test, there are 24 multiple-choice questions. It is not a good idea to memorise the questions as they will be different from those used in the actual test.

## IMPORTANT INFORMATION

As you read through the study material you may notice that some of the information is out of date. In the test you will only be asked about the information that is covered in this guide. You will not be tested on changes to the law or other regulations that are not mentioned in this guide.

## How are the chapters organised?

Each chapter presents the official study material from the handbook in short sections to make it easier for you to remember.
Each chapter follows the same format:

- **a brief introduction to help you identify the main points covered in the chapter;**
- **the study material from the Home Office handbook, including features to help you learn;**
- **revision questions and end of chapter checklist to help you check your progress as you go through the chapters;**
- **answers to the *Helping you learn* feature.**

## How is the study material presented?

The study material is clearly presented in boxes with a thick grey border so that it is easy to identify, read and remember. An example is below.

### Migration to Britain

Many people living in Britain today have their origin in other countries. They can trace their roots to regions throughout the world such as Europe, the Middle East, Africa, Asia and the Caribbean. In the distant past, invaders came to Britain, seized land and stayed. More recently people come to Britain to find safety, jobs and a better life.

## Which features are used in this guide?

### 1. Helping you learn
These are questions and activities relating to short sections of the study material. They are designed to help you to check your knowledge of the text as you work through it. Answers to these can be found at the end of each chapter.

### 2. Study tips
In addition to the study tips in Chapter 1, you will find more study tips included throughout the chapters. The tips will give you advice on how to remember the study material.

### 3.  Important information

This feature highlights important facts. For example, if you live in Wales, Scotland or Northern Ireland, you will need to read carefully the information that applies to your region as some of the test questions are likely to be specific to your region.

### 4.  Did you know?

Each chapter also includes *Did you know?* features. These give interesting facts and figures. You do not have to learn them as they will not be included in the test.

## SECTION 2  Who should take the test?

Not everyone needs to take the test to apply for British citizenship. There are two different routes depending on your level of English.

1.  **If your level of English is at ESOL Entry 3 or above, the *Life in the UK* test will be suitable for you. You will be able to take the test after you have read the study material in this guide and practised the test questions. If you are unsure whether your English skills are at the right level, you should complete the Assessment activity in Section 3 of this chapter.**

2.  **If your level of English is below ESOL Entry 3, you do not need to take the test. You will need to join an ESOL and citizenship course and achieve a *Skills for Life* qualification in speaking and listening.**

You do not need to take the test or follow an ESOL and citizenship course if you:

■  **are over 65;**

■  **have a long-term health condition;**

■  **have a cognitive learning difficulty;**

■  **have a physical disability that would prevent you from going to an ESOL class or taking the test.**

DID YOU KNOW?

**Did you know that over 100,000 people take the *Life in the UK* test every year?**

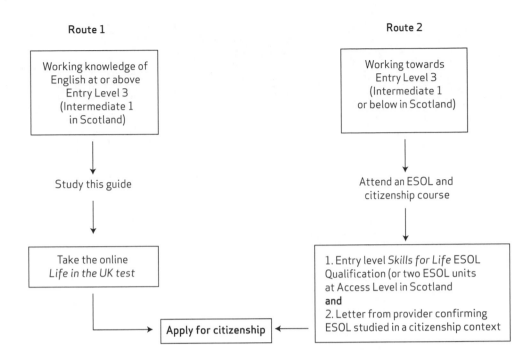

**Route 1**

Working knowledge of English at or above Entry Level 3 (Intermediate 1 in Scotland)

Study this guide

Take the online *Life in the UK test*

**Route 2**

Working towards Entry Level 3 (Intermediate 1 or below in Scotland)

Attend an ESOL and citizenship course

1. Entry level *Skills for Life* ESOL Qualification (or two ESOL units at Access Level in Scotland **and** 2. Letter from provider confirming ESOL studied in a citizenship context

Apply for citizenship

**Figure 1.1** Diagram to help you understand who the test is suitable for.

## SECTION 3 Assessment activity

The following activity is to help you assess whether the level of your reading is at Entry 3.

The text below is not from the *Life in the United Kingdom: A journey to citizenship* handbook, but is at a similar level. Like the handbook, it contains some more difficult specialist words.

Read the text and answer the questions. There is no time limit, but you should try not to take more than about 30 minutes. You should not use a dictionary.

The questions are to check your understanding of the language. They are like those you would have to answer in a *Skills for Life* ESOL test at Entry 3. They are *not* the kind of questions that are in the *Life in the UK* test.

**Figure 1.2** Factories send out carbon gases.

A. Climate change is one of the most serious problems facing the world today. The average temperature is rising each year all over the planet. One of the main reasons for this is that our cars, homes and factories send out harmful carbon gases. This makes the atmosphere of the earth hotter and damages our environment. It can lead to extreme weather conditions, such as flooding in places near rivers or the sea, or drought in hot countries. Every day, more and more people in the UK are 'going green' to tackle the problem of climate change. Here are some ideas about how you can help.

B. We burn coal, oil or gas to heat our homes or produce electricity. This causes carbon gas emissions that lead to climate change. About 80% of the energy you use at home goes on heating and hot water. You can make a big saving by turning your heating down and improving insulation, so that less heat is lost through the walls and roof. Try not to use more water than necessary. For example, if you have a shower, you will normally use less water than if you have a bath.

C. Car travel is one of the main causes of climate change. If you are buying a new car, make sure you choose a more efficient model that produces less carbon. This way, you will also save money on fuel and Vehicle Tax. You can reduce air pollution even more if you make fewer short journeys in your car. If you walk or cycle, it will also be good for your health. Try to use public transport where you can.

D. Producing, transporting and consuming food causes nearly 20% of our climate change effects. Buy food that is fresh and produced locally, as this normally uses less energy than food that has to be transported a long distance. The average UK household spends £424 a year on food that is thrown away. At rubbish tips, this produces methane, a gas that is very harmful to the environment. Cutting out food waste saves you money and helps the environment.

E. Reducing and recycling waste saves on the energy that is needed to make new paper, metal, glass and other items. Avoid waste in the first place, by buying items that can be reused. You can pass them on to somebody else when you have finished with them. Nearly two-thirds of all household rubbish can be recycled. Most local councils run recycling collections for paper, glass and plastics. You can take many other things, such as shoes, textiles and televisions, to a local recycling site.

F. There are now a lot of choices you can make when shopping that help take care of the environment. Keep your shopping bags and take some with you when you next go to the supermarket, rather than using new plastic bags every time. Appliances such as refrigerators and washing machines must, by law, have labels that explain how efficiently they use energy. Choose recycled products when buying items such as paper, kitchen rolls and toilet tissue.

*Source*: Adapted from material on Directgov, the website of the UK Government: www.direct.gov.uk

## Questions

### 1–5 The title of the text and paragraph headings are missing. Answer the following questions about this.

1. Which would be the most suitable title for the whole text?
   a   What is climate change?
   b   What you can do about climate change
   c   How you can save money
   d   Why you should recycle

2. For which paragraph would *Getting around* be a suitable heading?

3. For which paragraph would *Greener shopping* be a suitable heading?

4. For which paragraph would *Eating and drinking* be a suitable heading?

5. What is the main purpose of the text? Circle the correct answer.
   a   to advertise products
   b   to explain the law
   c   to give advice
   d   to express an opinion

### 6–10 Circle whether the following sentences are true or false, according to the text.

6. If you buy an energy-efficient car, you will pay less for your Vehicle Tax.
   T     F

7. Only a small amount of household rubbish can be recycled.
   T     F

8. Electrical products such as televisions and computers use most energy in the home.
   T     F

9. Food products that are transported a long distance can cause climate change.
   T     F

10. You can easily find out whether an electrical appliance uses energy efficiently.
    T     F

## 11–15 Answer the questions with one word only in the space provided.

11. In paragraph A, which word means *a period when there is not enough water?*

Answer_____

12. In paragraph C, which word means that *something works well?*

Answer_____

13. In paragraph D, which word means *using something?*

Answer_____

14. In paragraph E, which word means *material used in making clothes?*

Answer_____

15. In paragraph F, which word means *items of electrical equipment?*

Answer_____

## 16–20 Write the answer in the space provided.

16. What kind of gas is produced by waste food at rubbish tips?

Answer_____

17. What is one way of using less water in the home?

Answer_____

18. How do carbon gases cause climate change?

Answer_____

19. Apart from choosing an efficient model, how can you reduce the pollution caused by your car?

Answer_____

20. Name *two* kinds of waste that are collected for recycling by most local councils.

Answer_____

---

## Answers for the assessment activity

---

| | | |
|---|---|---|
| 1. | b | None of the other choices covers the whole text. |
| 2. | Paragraph C | *Getting around* is a phrase that means the same as *travelling*. |
| 3. | Paragraph F | The word *green* can mean *helping the environment*. |
| 4. | Paragraph D | Eating and drinking are ways of *consuming* food. |
| 5. | c | The text describes things you *can* do (but don't have to). |
| 6. | True | You will save money on fuel and *Vehicle Tax*. (Paragraph C) |
| 7. | False | *Nearly two-thirds* can be recycled. (E) |
| 8. | False | About *80% of energy* goes on *heating and hot water*. (B) |
| 9. | True | *Transportation* helps to cause *nearly 20%* of climate change effects. (D) |
| 10. | True | These appliances must have *labels* with this information. (F) |

11. drought
12. efficient
13. consuming
14. textiles
15. appliances

16. Methane (D)
17. You can have a shower instead of a bath. (B)
18. They make the atmosphere of the earth hotter. (A)
19. You can make fewer short journeys. (C)
20. Paper, glass, plastics (any two). Other things such as shoes, textiles and televisions might not be collected. You might have to take them to the recycling centre. (F)

Give one mark for each correct answer. If you scored 14 or more out of 20, your level of reading is probably at Entry 3 or above. If you scored less than 14, you may have difficulty with the language of the handbook and should consider getting advice and a more detailed *Skills for Life* ESOL assessment from a college or other provider.

To help you identify areas where you had particular problems:

■ Questions 1–5 are about understanding how the whole text is organised (and the meaning of some phrases).

■ Questions 6–10 are about understanding the meaning of individual sentences.

■ Questions 11–15 are about understanding the meanings of individual words and making an accurate guess if you don't know them.

■ Questions 16–20 are about finding specific information in the whole text.

# SECTION 4  Taking the test

This section contains some of the most frequently asked questions about the *Life in the UK* test.

## IMPORTANT INFORMATION

More detailed information about the test, including the type of questions you will be asked, tips to help you in the test and what to expect on the day of the test, are in Chapter 8 of this guide.

### Where can I take the test?
You can take the test at one of the many test centres around the UK.

### After booking the test, how long will I have to wait for a test appointment?
You will have to wait a minimum of seven days for the appointment, but it may be longer. When you have the date of your test you can plan your study time towards that goal.

### How do I find out where my local test centre is?
You can find this out from the *Life in the UK* test website **www.lifeintheuktest.gov.uk** or you can call the Helpline on 0800 0154245.

**How much does the test cost?**
The test costs £33.28 (including VAT).

**Do I have to take the test on a computer?**
The test is only available on a computer, but don't worry, you only need very basic computer skills.

**How many questions are in the test?**
There are 24 multiple-choice questions in the test.

**How many questions do I need to get right in order to pass?**
The pass mark is 75%, therefore you need to get 18 questions correct.

**How much time will I have?**
You will have 45 minutes to complete the test.

**If I live in Scotland, Wales or Northern Ireland will there be questions about my region?**
The test will include questions that ask you about the part of the UK where you live.

**What happens if I fail the test?**
Don't worry, you can take the test as many times as you need to.

**If I take the test again will I have the same questions?**
Questions are chosen at random from a selection of 400 questions, so it is unlikely you will have any of the same questions.

> **IMPORTANT** INFORMATION

All the test questions are multiple choice. This means that you do not need to be good at spelling to pass the *Life in the UK* test. You will not need to remember how to spell or pronounce any of the words in the study material, you will only need to recognise them.

# SECTION 5  Study tips

This section includes ideas and study tips to help you remember information quickly and effectively. Everyone learns differently, so choose the methods that work best for you.

## Planning your study time

If you are busy and find it difficult to make time to study, it will be easier if you plan your study time in advance. Try making a timetable and give yourself enough time before the test date so that you can remember the information you need to know without feeling rushed. If you do this and stick to it you will not feel as stressed.

Try to relax and not worry about the test, as it is more difficult to learn when you feel stressed. Even if the worst happens and you don't pass the test, you can always take it again.

Organise your study time into short periods and make sure that you take regular breaks. Studying for hours at a time without a break will make it hard for you to concentrate. If you are new to studying, start off trying 10–15 minutes at a time and slowly increase the time.

---

DID YOU KNOW?

**Did you know that it's important to drink plenty of water? Dehydration makes it difficult to concentrate.**

**Figure 1.3**

Learn to recognise when you need to take a break and try not to study for more than 45 minutes without a short rest.

People learn in different ways. Some people find it easier to study with music on, while other people find it distracting. Check where you plan to study – is it suitable for how you like to learn? If you do need a quiet place to study, try the local public library if there is nowhere suitable where you live.

Think about the best time for you to study. Some people find that they learn best in the morning and find it more difficult to study late at night when they are more tired. Some people work better at night. The important thing is that you study at a time when it is going to be most beneficial to you.

---

**DID YOU KNOW?**

**Did you know that talking about what you have learned and explaining it to someone else helps you to understand and remember the information?**

---

Think about how you learn best. Do you learn best by reading, making notes or drawing diagrams? Take these things into consideration when you are planning your studies.

Make sure you have all the equipment you will need, for example a notebook, pen, highlighters and a dictionary.

## Reading to remember

To pass the test you will have to read and remember detailed information. The following advice may help you.

- Get a feel for the section – read it quickly and ask yourself these questions.
    - Can I remember most of it?
    - What are the key points?

- Then read the section again in detail – you may need to do this several times to remember it. Then try the following.
    - Write the key points in your own words.
    - Check your notes against the passage.

■ Correct and amend your notes.

■ Make sure you have covered the key points of each paragraph.

Try to answer from memory the questions at the end of each section you have read. This will let you know what you have learned and what you are still unsure about.

DID YOU KNOW?

**Did you know that research shows that we quickly forget about 80% of what we read? If you do something active, such as taking notes or underlining important points, it helps you to remember the information.**

## Making notes

Notes will:

■ help you to remember what you are reading;

■ be useful for revision;

■ be shorter and quicker to read and learn.

There are two main ways you can make notes. You can either use a separate book or piece of paper or you can make notes in this guide.

The advantages of making notes in this guide are:

■ it's quick;

■ key phrases can be underlined or highlighted with a highlighter pen;

■ comments can be added in the margin.

The disadvantages of making notes in the guide are:

■ you haven't summarised points in your own words to help you understand and remember the information;

■ it is difficult to revise from these notes later as you will need to look through the whole guide.

If you decide to make notes separately, the following suggestions may help.

■ Read each section and decide what the main points are and write them on cards or pieces of paper. These are sometimes called flashcards.

■ Do not write too much detail and leave space between the notes so that they are easy to read and remember.

■ Some people find that highlighting the important points helps them to remember the information.

■ When you have made your notes, try putting the cards in places around your home where you can see them frequently, for example on your fridge door.

---

| DID YOU KNOW? |
| --- |

**Your brain carries on working during study breaks and at night so, if you don't remember information or facts straightaway, don't worry – your brain might still be processing the information.**

## Checking your understanding

After reading each section, decide what the main points are and try to describe them in your own words. If you do this you will be more likely to remember the information and able to answer revision questions.

The following tips may help you to remember the main points from the study material.

## Mnemonics

This is a very old method of helping you to remember lists. They do not need to make sense and can often be funny. For example, the simple mnemonic below:

**F**armers **A**ccess **T**elevision **A**nd **L**isten **D**aily could be used to learn the six counties of Northern Ireland:

**F**ermanagh, **A**rmagh, **T**yrone, **A**ntrim, **L**ondonderry, **D**own

The best mnemonics are usually personal ones that you make up when you are learning. If possible, relate them to the information you are trying to remember.

You can also use pictures in your mind to help you remember the information. Many people find that imagery (seeing the picture in your head) helps to improve their memory. Why not try it? It may work for you.

For example, try imagining a Christmas tree with the number 25 on it to help you remember that Christmas Day is 25 December.

**Figure 1.4**

## Spider diagrams

If you are a visual learner, spider diagrams or mind maps might work well for you. They can be an effective way of linking facts together. For example, the spider diagram on page 20 shows the four regions of the UK and some of the cities in each of the regions.

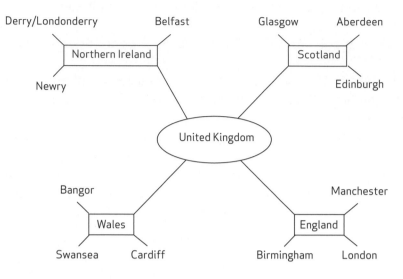

**Figure 1.5**   Spider diagram to show cities in the UK.

## Diagrams

Diagrams are very useful tools. They can bring information together and give you practice at reorganising what you have read. They can quickly remind you of details, especially if you made the diagram yourself.

Try making a sketch or diagram on cards. These can then be used as effective revision tools and will be quicker than rereading the study material or written notes.

## Tips to help you remember dates

You are not alone if you find dates and numbers hard to remember. Many people find them particularly difficult. If you do, see if the following helps.

■ Try identifying dates with personal information, such as the date of birth of a friend or family member, or a house number where you used to live. For example, to help you remember that women over 21 were given the right to vote in 1928, you could link this date to when women in your country received the right to vote.

■ Try imagining numbers as pictures, for example a number 2 as a swan.

■ Try repeating dates to a musical beat.

## Dictionary skills

If you use a dictionary to look up every word that you don't understand it will slow you down and you may start to feel frustrated. See if you can work out the meaning of the word from reading the sentence. If you can't, ask yourself if you need to know the meaning of the word to understand the overall meaning of the sentence or idea.

Remember, you don't need to know the meaning of every word you read to be able to understand the overall meaning.

## Revision

Regular revision will improve your confidence. As well as the *Helping you learn* questions, revision questions are also included at the end of each section. Make sure that you try to answer the questions to check that you can remember the information.

If possible, ask a friend or relative if they can help you by asking you questions from this study guide or by making up questions directly from your notes. This is a good way to check your knowledge. They may also be interested in knowing some of the information you have learned as many people born in the UK do not know all the answers.

## IMPORTANT INFORMATION

Do not memorise the questions in this book. The questions are to help you check your understanding of the study materials and to help you see if you are ready to take the test. The test questions will not be the same.

# CHAPTER 2

# A changing society

In this chapter you will read the official study material and learn about how British society has changed in recent history.

To make it easier for you to learn the information, the chapter is divided into four sections.

**Section 1**  Migration to Britain.

**Section 2**  The changing role of women.

**Section 3**  Children, family and young people.

**Section 4**  Revision questions and end of chapter checklist.

## IMPORTANT INFORMATION

Remember that you will need to read all the official study material. Any of the information could be included in the test questions.

You may find some of these words difficult. To help you, some of these are included in the glossary in Chapter 7. It may also be helpful to have a dictionary available to check and make a note of any other words you do not understand.

You may find the following two terms confusing. To help with this, dictionary definitions are given.

Migration – (noun) moving to settle in a new area in order to find work.

Migrate – (verb).

Immigration – (noun) coming to live permanently in a foreign country.

Immigrate – (verb).

# SECTION 1 Migration to Britain

In this section you will read about:

- the history of people coming to live permanently in Britain;
- the reasons people came to Britain;
- the countries they came from;
- the types of jobs they came to do.

**Figure 2.1**  The UK encouraged immigration after the Second World War for economic reasons. Some of the first immigrants from Jamaica arrive at Tilbury, London, on board the *Empire Windrush*. (Photo by Popperfoto/Getty Images)

STUDY TIP

You may find it easier to read each section through once quickly to get the overall meaning of it and then concentrate on reading the study material one paragraph at a time. You may need to read the paragraph several times.

In this chapter there are lots of dates that you will need to remember for the test. To help you with your revision there is a timeline in Figure 2.2 (page 27) of the important dates that you will need to learn for the section on migration.

For more tips to help you remember dates, why not have a look at the study tips in Chapter 1?

## **IMPORTANT** INFORMATION

**United Kingdom or Great Britain?**

**Throughout the study materials the terms United Kingdom (UK), Great Britain (Britain) and British Isles are used. There is some confusion about the correct meanings and use of these terms.**

**The United Kingdom consists of four countries:**

 **England;**

■ **Scotland;**

■ **Wales;**

■ **Northern Ireland (the rest of Ireland is an independent country).**

**These four countries came together to form a union called the** *United Kingdom of Great Britain and Northern Ireland* **, and this is the official name of the United Kingdom.**

**The name 'Britain' or 'Great Britain' refers only to England, Scotland and Wales, and does not include Northern Ireland. The**

adjective 'British' usually refers to everyone in the UK, including Northern Ireland.

There are also several islands that are closely linked to the United Kingdom but do not form part of it. These are the Channel Islands and the Isle of Man. They have kept their own institutions of government and are called 'Crown Territories'.

## Migration to Britain

Many people living in Britain today have their origin in other countries. They can trace their roots to regions throughout the world, such as Europe, the Middle East, Africa, Asia and the Caribbean. In the distant past, invaders came to Britain, seized land and stayed. More recently, people have come to Britain to find safety, jobs and a better life.

Britain is proud of its tradition of offering safety to people who are escaping persecution and hardship. For example, in the 16th and 18th centuries, the Huguenots (French Protestants) came to Britain to escape religious persecution in France. In the mid-1840s there was a terrible famine in Ireland and many Irish people migrated to Britain. Many Irish men became labourers and helped to build canals and railways across Britain.

From 1880 to 1910, a large number of Jewish people came to Britain to escape racist attacks (called 'pogroms') in what was then called the Russian Empire and from the countries now called Poland, Ukraine and Belarus.

### DID YOU KNOW?

Did you know that over one million Irish people died in the potato famine of the mid-1840s and two million emigrated to Britain and the USA?

**2.1**   Can you give two examples of the types of work Irish migrant workers did in the mid-1840s?

**2.2**   Is the following statement TRUE or FALSE?
The Huguenots came to Britain to escape religious persecution in France.

When you have completed these questions you can check your answers at the end of the chapter.

# Migration since 1945

After the Second World War (1939–45), there was a huge task of rebuilding Britain. There were not enough people to do the work, so the British government encouraged workers from Ireland and other parts of Europe to come to the UK to help with the reconstruction. In 1948, people from the West Indies were also invited to come to work.

During the 1950s, there was still a shortage of labour in the UK. The UK encouraged immigration in the 1950s for economic reasons and many industries advertised for workers from overseas. For example, centres were set up in the West Indies to recruit people to drive buses. Textile and engineering firms from the north of England and the Midlands sent agents to India and Pakistan to find workers. For about 25 years, people from the West Indies, India, Pakistan, and later Bangladesh, travelled to work and settle in Britain.

The number of people migrating from these areas fell in the late 1960s and the early 1970s because the Government passed new laws to restrict immigration to Britain, although immigrants from 'old' Commonwealth countries such as Australia, New Zealand and Canada did not have to face such strict controls.

During this time, however, the UK was able to help a large number of refugees. In 1972, the UK accepted thousands of people of Indian origin who had been forced to leave Uganda. Another programme to help people from Vietnam was introduced in the late 1970s. Since 1979, more than 25,000 refugees from South East Asia have been allowed to settle in the UK.

In the 1980s, the largest immigrant groups were from the United States, Australia, South Africa and New Zealand. In the early 1990s, groups from the former Soviet Union came to Britain looking for a new and safer way of life. Since 1994, there has been a global rise in mass migration for both political and economic reasons.

## HELPING YOU LEARN

**2.3** After the Second World War, why did the government encourage workers from Ireland and other parts of Europe to come to the UK?

**2.4** Which of the following statements is correct?

**A.** In the late 1960s and early 1970s, the government restricted immigration to Britain from countries such as Australia, New Zealand and Canada.

**B.** In the late 1960s and early 1970s, the government restricted immigration to Britain from the West Indies, India, Pakistan and Bangladesh.

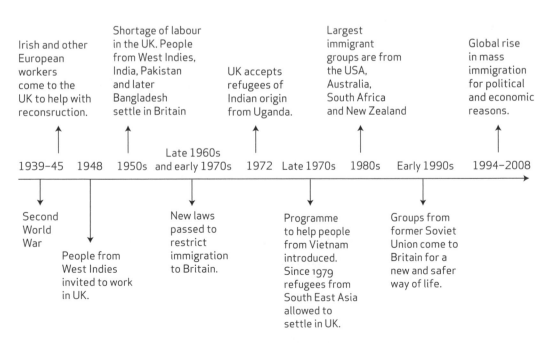

**Figure 2.2** Timeline to help you remember the dates in this section on migration.

**checklist** – Migration to Britain

Now you have read Section 1, can you remember the following?

- ■ **The main immigrant groups that have come to the UK.**
- ■ **Why people came to the UK.**
- ■ **Why Britain wanted and needed new immigrants.**

# SECTION 2 The changing role of women

In this section you will read about:

- ■ **women's rights since the 19th century, including the Suffragette movement;**
- ■ **the role of women in Britain today and their place in the workforce;**
- ■ **the discrimination that women faced entering and engaging in the workplace and in education.**

DID YOU KNOW?

**Did you know that, in a horse race in 1913, Emily Davison, who was a member of the Suffragettes, threw herself under the King's horse and was killed? She did this to make people more aware of the Suffragettes.**

STUDY TIP

To help you remember the dates in this section on the changing role of women, why not make your own timeline?

Look back at the one in Figure 2.2 if you want to see an example.

For more ideas to help you remember dates, look in the study skills section of Chapter 1.

# The changing role of women

In 19th-century Britain, families were usually large and in many poorer homes men, women and children all contributed towards the family income. Although they made an important economic contribution, women in Britain had fewer rights than men. Until 1857, a married woman had no right to divorce her husband. Until 1882, when a woman got married, her earnings, property and money automatically belonged to her husband.

In the late 19th and early 20th centuries, an increasing number of women campaigned and demonstrated for greater rights and, in particular, the right to vote. They became known as 'Suffragettes'. These protests decreased during the First World War because women joined in the war effort and therefore did a much greater variety of work than they had before. When the First World War ended in 1918, women over the age of 30 were finally given the right to vote and to stand for election to Parliament. It was not until 1928 that women won the right to vote at 21, at the same age as men.

Despite these improvements, women still faced discrimination in the workplace. For example, it was quite common for employers to ask women to leave their jobs when they got married. Many jobs were closed to women and it was difficult for women to enter universities. During the 1960s and 1970s, there was an increasing pressure from women for equal rights. Parliament passed new laws giving women the right to equal pay and prohibiting employers from discriminating against women because of their sex (see also Chapter 6).

## HELPING YOU LEARN

**2.5** Is the following statement TRUE or FALSE?
Until 1917, a married woman had no right to divorce her husband.

**2.6** Without looking at the text, can you remember in which year women were first granted the right to vote at the age of 30?

**Figure 2.3**
Women in Britain today make up
51% of the population and 45%
of the workforce.

# Women in Britain today

Women in Britain today make up 51% of the population and 45% of
the workforce. These days girls leave school, on average, with better
qualifications than boys and there are now more women than men at
university.

Employment opportunities for women are now much greater than
they were in the past. Although women continue to be employed in
traditional female areas such as healthcare, teaching, secretarial and
retail work, there is strong evidence that attitudes are changing, and
women are now active in a much wider range of work than before.
Research shows that very few people today believe that women in
Britain should stay at home and not go out to work. Today, almost
three-quarters of women with school-age children are in paid work.

In most households, women continue to have the main
responsibility for childcare and housework. There is evidence that there
is now greater equality in homes and that more men are taking some
responsibility for raising the family and doing housework. Despite this
progress, many people believe that more needs to be done to achieve
greater equality for women. There are still examples of discrimination
against women, particularly in the workplace, despite the laws that exist
to prevent it. Women still do not always have the same access to
promotion and better-paid jobs. The average hourly pay rate for women
is 20% less than for men and, after leaving university, most women still
earn less than men.

## HELPING YOU LEARN

**2.7**  Choose the correct words from this list to complete the statement.

**A.**  a quarter          **B.**  a half          **C.**  three-quarters

Today, almost .......................... of women with school-age children are in paid work.

**2.8**  Is the following statement TRUE or FALSE?
The average hourly rate of pay for women is 15% less than for men.

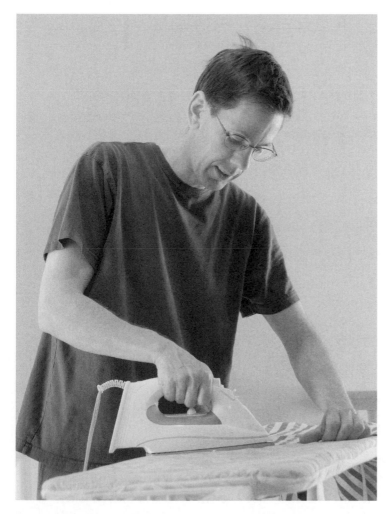

**Figure 2.4**  There is evidence that more men are taking some responsibility for raising the family and doing housework.

---

**checklist** – The changing role of women

---

Now you have read Section 2, can you remember the following?

■ How women have become more active in education, the workplace and politics.

■ The differences that have developed in how women contribute in their more traditional family roles.

■ When women aged over 30 were first given the right to vote.

■ When women were given equal voting rights with men.

■ Some of the important developments to create equal rights in the workplace.

# SECTION 3  Children, family and young people

In this section you will read about:

■ the lifestyle patterns of children and young people;

■ how young people are educated and the examinations they take;

■ common part-time jobs for young people;

■ the employment laws relating to young people;

■ the health hazards young people face in today's society.

## Children, family and young people

In the UK, there are almost 15 million children and young people up to the age of 19. This is almost one-quarter of the UK population.

Over the last 20 years, family patterns in Britain have been transformed because of changing attitudes towards divorce and separation. Today, 65% of children live with both birth parents, almost 25% live in lone-parent families, and 10% live within a stepfamily. Most children in Britain receive weekly pocket money from their parents and many get extra money for doing jobs around the house.

Children in the UK do not play outside the home as much as they did in the past. Part of the reason for this is increased home entertainment, such as television, videos and computers. There is also increased concern for children's safety and there are many stories in the newspapers about child molestation by strangers, but there is no evidence that this kind of danger is increasing.

Young people have different identities, interests and fashions from older people. Many young people move away from their family homes when they become adults, but this varies from one community to another.

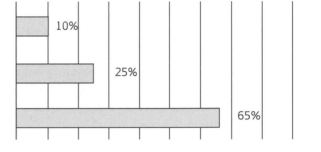

**Figure 2.5** Family living patterns in Britain.

HELPING YOU LEARN

2.9  In the UK, how many children and young people are there up to the age of 19?
2.10  Without looking at the text, can you give two reasons why children do not play outside as much now as they used to?

STUDY TIP

You may find the next section on education complicated. To help you remember it, try writing out the key points in your own words and remember to keep your notes short. If you are not sure of the best way to do this, there are some ideas in the study skills section in Chapter 1.

There is also a summary of this section in Figure 2.6 on page 35 to help you remember the details.

# Education

The law states that children between the ages of 5 and 16 must attend school. The tests that pupils take are very important, and in England and Scotland children take national tests in English, mathematics and science when they are 7, 11 and 14 years old. (In Wales, teachers assess children's progress when they are 7 and 11, and they take a national test at the age of 14.) The tests give important information about children's progress and achievement, the subjects they are doing well in and the areas where they need extra help.

Most young people take the General Certificate of Secondary Education (GCSE), or, in Scotland, Scottish Qualifications Authority (SQA) Standard Grade examinations when they are 16. At 17 and 18, many take vocational qualifications, General Certificates of Education at an Advanced Level (AGCEs), AS level units or Higher/Advanced Higher Grades in Scotland. Schools and colleges will expect good GCSE or SQA Standard Grade results before allowing a student to enrol on an AGCE or Scottish Higher/Advanced Higher course.

AS Levels are Advanced Subsidiary qualifications gained by completing three AS units. Three AS units are considered as one-half of an AGCE. In the second part of the course, three more AS units can be studied to complete the AGCE qualification.

Many people refer to AGCEs by the old name of A Levels. AGCEs are the traditional route for entry to higher education courses, but many higher education students enter with different kinds of qualifications.

One in three young people now go on to higher education at college or university. Some young people defer their university entrance for a year and take a 'gap year'. This year out of education often includes voluntary work and travel overseas. Some young people work to earn and save money to pay for their university fees and living expenses.

People over 16 years of age may also choose to study at Colleges of Further Education or Adult Education Centres. There is a wide range of academic and vocational courses available as well as courses which develop leisure interests and skills. Contact your local college for details.

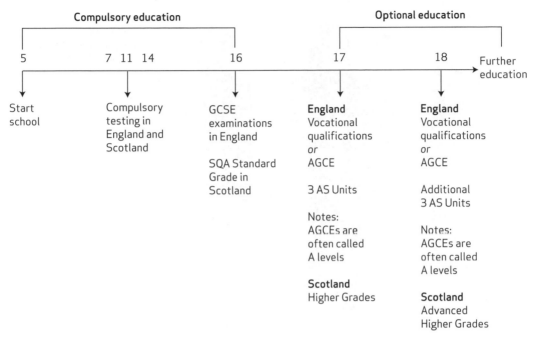

**Figure 2.6** Summary of the education process in the UK.

## HELPING YOU LEARN

**2.11** By what name do many people refer to the AGCEs?

**2.12** Which one of the following is the Scottish equivalent to the General Certificate of Secondary Education (GCSE)?

**A.** Standard Grade

**B.** Higher/Advanced Higher

## Work

It is common for young people to have a part-time job while they are still at school. It is thought there are two million children at work at any one time. The most common jobs are newspaper delivery and work in supermarkets and newsagents. Many parents believe that part-time work helps children to become more independent as well as providing them (and sometimes their families) with extra income.

There are laws about the age when children can take up paid work (usually not before 14), the type of work they can do and the number of hours they can work (see **www.worksmart.org.uk** for more information).

It is very important to note that there are concerns for the safety of children who work illegally or who are not properly supervised and the employment of children is strictly controlled by law.

**Figure 2.8** The most common jobs for young people are newspaper delivery and work in supermarkets and newsagents.

HELPING YOU LEARN

**2.13** Which of these statements is correct?
  **A.** There are approximately two million children at work in the UK at any one time.
  **B.** There are approximately four million children at work in the UK at any one time.

# Health hazards

Many parents worry that children may misuse drugs and addictive substances.

## Smoking
Although cigarette smoking is slowly falling in the adult population, more young people are smoking, and more school-age girls smoke than boys. From 1 October 2007 it is illegal to sell tobacco products to anyone under 18 years old. Smoking is generally not allowed in public buildings and work places throughout the UK.

### Alcohol

Young people under the age of 18 are not allowed to buy alcohol in Britain, but there is concern about the age some young people start drinking alcohol and the amount of alcohol they drink at one time, known as 'binge drinking'. It is illegal to be drunk in public and there are now more penalties to help control this problem, including on-the-spot fines.

### Illegal drugs

As in most countries, it is illegal to possess drugs such as heroin, cocaine, ecstasy, amphetamines and cannabis. Current statistics show that half of all young adults, and about a third of the population as a whole, have used illegal drugs at one time or another.

There is a strong link between the use of hard drugs (e.g. crack cocaine and heroin) and crime, and also hard drugs and mental illness. The misuse of drugs has a huge social and financial cost for the country. This is a serious issue and British society needs to find an effective way of dealing with the problem.

---

### HELPING YOU LEARN

**2.14** At what age can young people buy tobacco products?
**2.15** Is the following statement TRUE or FALSE?
   Half of all young adults have used illegal drugs at one time or another.

---

## Young people's political and social attitudes

Young people in Britain can vote in elections from the age of 18. In the 2001 general election, however, only 1 in 5 first-time voters used their vote. There has been a great debate over the reasons for this. Some researchers think that one reason is that young people are not interested in the political process.

Although most young people show little interest in party politics, there is strong evidence that many are interested in specific political issues such as the environment and cruelty to animals.

In 2003 a survey of young people in England and Wales showed that they believe the five most important issues in Britain were crime, drugs, war/terrorism, racism and health. The same survey asked young people about their participation in political and community events. They found that 86% of young people had taken part in some form of community event over the past year, and 50% had taken part in fund-raising or collecting money for charity. Similar results have been found in surveys in Scotland and Northern Ireland. Many children first get involved in these activities while at school, where they study Citizenship as part of the National Curriculum.

**Figure 2.9**  One in five young people voted in the 2001 general election.

HELPING YOU LEARN

**2.16** How old do young people have to be to vote in elections in Britain?

| **checklist** – Children, family and young children |
| --- |

Now you have read Section 3, can you remember the following?

■ The proportion of all young people who go on to higher education.

■ Lifestyle patterns of children and young people (e.g. pocket money, leaving home on reaching adulthood).

■ Changing family patterns and attitudes to changing family patterns (e.g. divorce).

■ That education in Britain is free and compulsory, and that there is compulsory testing (in England and Scotland) at ages 7, 11 and 14; there are also GCSE and/or vocational exams at 16; and Advanced Level exams (A and AS) at ages 17 and 18.

■ That there is a government target that half of all young people undertake higher education.

■ That there are strict laws regarding the employment of children.

■ That there are important health concerns and laws relating to children and young people, and smoking, alcohol and drugs.

■ That young people are eligible to vote in elections from the age of 18.

■ The challenges of young people today.

■ Make sure that you have read and understood the political and social attitudes of young people.

# SECTION 4 Revision questions and end of chapter checklist

Now you have finished reading the official study material, try to answer the following questions to see how much of Chapter 2 you can remember. If you are unsure of the answers, check your notes and refer back to the text before looking at the answers at the end of the book.

**IMPORTANT** INFORMATION

Remember that these are revision questions and not in the same format as the actual test.

## Revision questions for Chapter 2

1. What are the main reasons migrants come to the UK?

Answer_____

2. Why was there a fall in the number of people migrating to the UK from the West Indies, India, Pakistan and Bangladesh in the late 1960s?

Answer_____

3. In the 1950s, why were people encouraged to come and live permanently in the UK?

Answer_____

4. When were women given equal voting rights with men?

Answer_____

5. What were women called who campaigned for greater rights for women in the late 19th and early 20th centuries?

Answer_____

6. Are there more women or men at university today?

Answer_____

7. What percentage of children live with both their parents?

Answer_____

8. Why do children play outside less today than they did in the past?

Answer_____

9. Between which ages must children attend school?

Answer_____

10. What type of qualifications do many young people aged 17 and 18 take in the UK?

Answer_____

11. What proportion of young people stay in education after 18?

Answer_____

12. At what age can children usually start part-time work?

Answer_____

13. At what age can young people legally buy tobacco products and alcohol in Britain?

Answer_____

14. At what age can young people vote in the UK?

Answer_____

The correct answers are at the back of this book.

**End of Chapter 2 checklist**

Now that you have come to the end of Chapter 2, tick the boxes when you have:

■ read the study material;                                                    ☐

■ made short notes to help you with your revision;                            ☐

■ made a note and checked words that you do not
  understand;                                                                 ☐

■ completed the *Helping you learn* and revision questions
  and checked your answers;                                                   ☐

■ gone back and read again the sections for the
  questions you got wrong.                                                    ☐

Well done, you have now finished Chapter 2 of the study material and are ready to move on to Chapter 3.

---

## Answers to *Helping you learn* questions for Chapter 2

---

2.1   Building canals and railways
2.2   True
2.3   Shortage of labour
2.4   B
2.5   False – it's 1857
2.6   1918
2.7   C
2.8   False – it's 20%
2.9   15 million
2.10  Increased home entertainment
      Increased concern for children's safety
2.11  A Levels
2.12  A
2.13  A
2.14  18
2.15  True
2.16  18

# CHAPTER 3

# The United Kingdom today: a profile

In this chapter you will read the official study material and learn about British society. You will also read about the different groups of people that live in the UK and find out about how their traditions, customs, religions and ethnic backgrounds differ in different parts of the country. You will read about the four nations that make up the United Kingdom – these are Wales, Scotland, England and Northern Ireland.

To make it easier for you to remember the information, the chapter is divided into five sections.

**Section 1** Population.

**Section 2** The nations and regions of the UK.

**Section 3** Religion.

**Section 4** Customs and traditions.

**Section 5** Revision questions and end of chapter checklist.

## IMPORTANT INFORMATION

Throughout this chapter you will need to know about the four nations that make up the United Kingdom. You may find it confusing as these are sometimes referred to as countries, regions or nations.

These are:

- Wales;
- Scotland;
- England;
- Northern Ireland.

**Figure 3.1**
The four nations of
the United Kingdom.

# SECTION 1  Population

In this section you will read about:

■ the population of the UK;

■ the census;

■ the regions of Britain;

■ the different ethnic groups within the UK.

## Population

In 2005 the population of the United Kingdom was just under 60 million people.

*UK population 2005*

| | | |
|---|---|---|
| England | (84% of the population) | 50.1 million |
| Scotland | (8% of the population) | 5.1 million |
| Wales | (5% of the population) | 2.9 million |
| N. Ireland | (3% of the population) | 1.7 million |
| Total UK | | 59.8 million |

*Source*: National Statistics

The population has grown by 7.7% since 1971, and growth has been faster in more recent years. Although the general population in the UK has increased in the last 20 years, in some areas such as the North-East and North-West of England there has been a decline.

Both the birth rate and the death rate are falling and, as a result, the UK now has an ageing population. For instance, there are more people over 60 than children under 16. There is also a record number of people aged 85 and over.

**Figure 3.2**
In 2005 the population of the UK was just under 60 million.

UK birth and death rates decreasing.

Population age increasing

**Figure 3.3** Age trends in the UK.

## DID YOU KNOW?

**Did you know that, in 1901, the population of the UK was 38 million and that it is expected to rise to 62 million by 2021?**
*Source*: A Century of Change: Trends in UK Statistics since 1900 (1999), House of Commons research paper 99/111

## HELPING YOU LEARN

**3.1** Using the study material to help you, write in the spaces below the population of each region in the UK.

England .................... million     Scotland ............................... million
Wales ....................... million     Northern Ireland .................... million

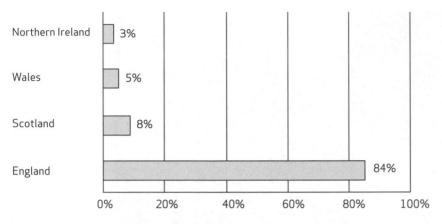

Figure 3.4 Percentage of the UK population for each nation of the UK.

## The census

A census is a count of the whole population. It also collects statistics on topics such as age, place of birth, occupation, ethnicity, housing, health and marital status.

A census has been taken every ten years since 1801, except during the Second World War. The next census will take place in 2011.

During a census, a form is delivered to every household in the country. This form asks for detailed information about each member of the household and by law must be completed. The information remains confidential and anonymous; it can only be released to the public after 100 years, when many people researching their family history find it very useful. General census information is used to identify population trends and to help planning. More information about the census, the census form and statistics from previous censuses can be found at **www.statistics.gov.uk/census**.

### HELPING YOU LEARN

**3.2**    Which of these statements is correct?
   **A**. The census is taken every 10 years.
   **B**. The census is taken every 15 years.
**3.3**    Look at Figure 3.5 and add TWO other topics that are collected in the census.

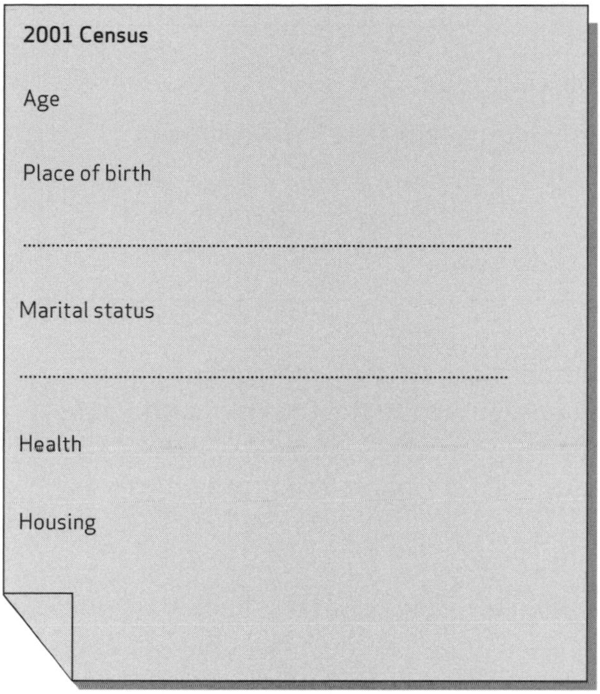

**Figure 3.5**

2001 Census

Age

Place of birth

.....................................................................

Marital status

.....................................................................

Health

Housing

# Ethnic diversity

The UK population is ethnically diverse and is changing rapidly, especially in large cities such as London, so it is not always easy to get an exact picture of the ethnic origin of all the population from census statistics. Each of the four countries of the UK (England, Wales, Scotland and Northern Ireland) has different customs, attitudes and histories.

People of Indian, Pakistani, Chinese, Black Caribbean, Black African, Bangladeshi and mixed ethnic descent make up 8.3% of the UK population. Today about half the members of these communities were born in the United Kingdom.

There are also considerable numbers of people resident in the UK who are of Irish, Italian, Greek and Turkish Cypriot, Polish, Australian, Canadian, New Zealand and American descent. Large numbers have also arrived since 2004 from the new East European member states of the European Union. These groups are not identified separately in the census statistics in the table on page 50.

| HELPING YOU LEARN |
|---|

**3.4** Is the following statement TRUE or FALSE?
England, Scotland, Wales and Northern Ireland have different
customs, attitudes and histories.

| STUDY TIP |
|---|

To help you remember the countries from where large numbers of
people have migrated and have now settled in the UK, try making your
own list.

Remember to check the study skills in Chapter 1 for other tips.

## UK population 2001

|  | Million | UK population % |
|---|---|---|
| *White* | 54.2 | 92 |
| (including people of European, | | |
| Australian, American descent) | | |
| Mixed | 0.7 | 1.2 |
| *Asian or Asian British* | | |
| Indian | 1.1 | 1.8 |
| Pakistani | 0.7 | 1.3 |
| Bangladeshi | 0.3 | 0.5 |
| Other Asian | 0.2 | 0.4 |
| *Black or Black British* | | |
| Black Caribbean | 0.6 | 1.0 |
| Black African | 0.5 | 0.8 |
| Black other | 0.1 | 0.2 |
| *Chinese* | 0.2 | 0.4 |
| *Other* | 0.2 | 0.4 |

*Source*: National Statistics from the 2001 census

**Where do the largest ethnic minority groups live?**

The figures from the 2001 census show that most members of the large ethnic minority groups in the UK live in England, where they make up 9% of the total population. About 45% of all ethnic minority people live in the London area, where they form nearly one-third of the population (29%). Other areas of England with large ethnic minority populations are the West Midlands, the South East, the North West, and Yorkshire and Humberside.

**Proportion of ethnic minority groups in the countries of the UK**

| | | | |
|---|---|---|---|
| England | 9% | Wales | 2% |
| Scotland | 2% | Northern Ireland | less than 1% |

---

HELPING YOU LEARN

**3.5**  Can you remember TWO areas in England with a large ethnic minority population?

**3.6**  Look at the map in Figure 3.6 on page 52 and write the percentage of ethnic minority groups against each region in the UK. You may need to reread the study material to find this information.

**3.7**  Identify where London is on the map and write the percentage of all ethnic minority people who live in the London area.

---

**checklist** – Population

Now you have read Section 1, can you remember the following?

■ **Information, including facts and figures, about the UK population.**

■ **The size of the UK population.**

■ **The population of England, Scotland, Wales and Northern Ireland.**

■ **The purpose of the census and what information is collected.**

**Figure 3.6**

Scotland .......... %

Northern Ireland
less than .......... %

England .......... %

.......... % of all ethnic
minority people
live in London

Wales .......... %

■ How often the census is carried out and when the next one will take place.

■ The proportion of different groups within the UK and where they are located.

# SECTION 2  The nations and regions of the UK

In this section you will read about:

■ the size of the country;

■ the regional differences in the UK;

■ the different dialects and languages that are spoken.

# The nations and regions of the UK

The UK is a medium-sized country. The longest distance on the mainland, from John O'Groats on the north coast of Scotland to Land's End in the south-west corner of England, is about 870 miles (approximately 1,400 kilometres). Most of the population lives in towns and cities.

There are many variations in culture and language in the different parts of the United Kingdom. This is seen in differences in architecture, in some local customs, in types of food, and especially in language. The English language has many accents and dialects. These are a clear indication of regional differences in the UK. Well-known dialects in England are Geordie (Tyneside), Scouse (Liverpool) and Cockney (London). Many other languages in addition to English are spoken in the UK, especially in multicultural cities.

In Wales, Scotland and Northern Ireland, people speak different varieties and dialects of English. In Wales, too, an increasing number of people speak Welsh, which is taught in schools and universities. In Scotland, Gaelic is spoken in some parts of the Highlands and Islands, and in Northern Ireland a few people speak Irish Gaelic. Some of the dialects of English spoken in Scotland show the influence of the old Scottish language, Scots. One of the dialects spoken in Northern Ireland is called Ulster Scots.

HELPING YOU LEARN

**3.8**  Look at the map in Figure 3.7 and write the languages and dialects spoken in each of the nations and some of the areas of the UK. Look back at the text to help you.

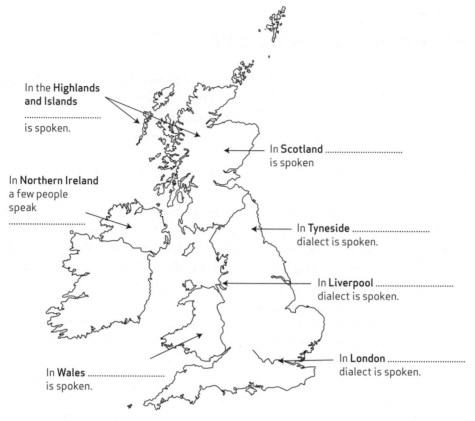

In the **Highlands and Islands**
..................
is spoken.

In **Scotland** ................................
is spoken

In **Northern Ireland** a few people speak
..................

In **Tyneside** ................................
dialect is spoken.

In **Liverpool** ................................
dialect is spoken.

In **London** ................................
dialect is spoken.

In **Wales** ................................
is spoken.

**Figure 3.7**

---

**checklist** – The nations and regions of the UK

Now you have read Section 2, can you remember the following?

■ **Which languages other than English are spoken in Wales, Scotland and Northern Ireland.**

■ **Some of the ways you can identify regional differences in the UK.**

# SECTION 3 Religion

In this section you will read about:

- the different religions in the UK;
- the structure of Christian churches in the UK and the role of the king or queen within the Church;
- 'bank holidays' and public holidays, and the patron saints.

## Religion

Although the UK is historically a Christian society, everyone has the legal right to practise the religion of their choice. In the 2001 census, just over 75% said they had a religion: seven out of ten of these were Christians. There were also a considerable number of people who followed other religions. Although many people in the UK said they held religious beliefs, currently only around 10% of the population attend religious services. More people attend services in Scotland and Northern Ireland than in England and Wales. In London the number of people who attend religious services is increasing.

| Religions in the UK | % |
|---|---|
| Christian (10% of whom are Roman Catholic) | 71.6 |
| Muslim | 2.7 |
| Hindu | 1.0 |
| Sikh | 0.6 |
| Jewish | 0.5 |
| Buddhist | 0.3 |
| Other | 0.3 |
| Total All | 77.0 |
| No religion | 15.5 |
| Not stated | 7.3 |

*Source*: National Statistics from the 2001 census

HELPING YOU LEARN

**3.9**   What percentage of the population currently attends religious services?

**3.10**   Is the following statement TRUE or FALSE?
More people attend services in Scotland and Northern Ireland than in England and Wales.

## The Christian churches

In England there is a constitutional link between Church and State. The official Church of the state is the Church of England. The Church of England is called the Anglican Church in other countries and the Episcopal Church in Scotland and in the USA. The Church of England is a Protestant church and has existed since the Reformation in the 1530s. The king or queen (the monarch) is the head, or Supreme Governor, of the Church of England. The monarch is not allowed to marry anyone who is not Protestant. The spiritual leader of the Church of England is the Archbishop of Canterbury. The monarch has the right to select the Archbishop and other senior church officials, but usually the choice is made by the Prime Minister and a committee appointed by the Church. Several Church of England bishops sit in the House of Lords (see Chapter 4). The Church of Scotland is Presbyterian, national and free from state control. It has no bishops and is governed for spiritual purposes by a series of courts, so its most senior representative is the Moderator (chairperson) of its annual General Assembly. There is no established Church in Wales or in Northern Ireland.

Other Protestant Christian groups in the UK are Baptists, Presbyterians, Methodists and Quakers. About 10% of Christians are Roman Catholic (40% in Northern Ireland).

**3.11**  Who is the spiritual leader of the Church of England?
**3.12**  Read the statements below and decide which TWO are correct.
   **A**  15% of Christians are Roman Catholic.
   **B**  10% of Christians are Roman Catholic.
   **C**  45% of Christians in Northern Ireland are Roman Catholic.
   **D**  40% of Christians in Northern Ireland are Roman Catholic.

STUDY TIP

To help you remember the information about the Church of England, there is a summary in the form of a spider diagram in Figure 3.8. You may find it helpful to make your own spider diagrams to help you remember other information in the study material.

If you find that spider diagrams don't work for you, you could try making short notes instead.

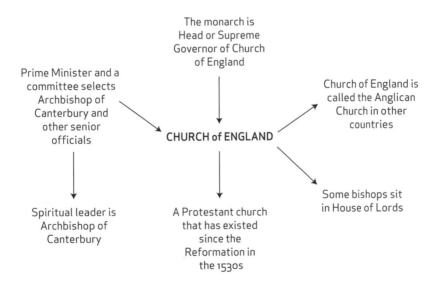

**Figure 3.8** Summary of information about the Church of England.

## Patron saints

England, Scotland, Wales and Northern Ireland each have a national saint called a patron saint. Each saint has a feast day. In the past these were celebrated as holy days when many people had a day off work. Today these are not public holidays except for 17 March in Northern Ireland.

**Patron saints' days**

| | |
|---|---|
| St David's day, Wales | 1 March |
| St Patrick's day, Northern Ireland | 17 March |
| St George's day, England | 23 April |
| St Andrew's day, Scotland | 30 November |

There are four 'bank holidays' and four other public holidays a year (most people call all these holidays bank holidays).

DID YOU KNOW?

**Did you know that, in Wales on St David's day, many people wear a daffodil because it is the national symbol of Wales?**

HELPING YOU LEARN

**3.13**   Without looking at the text, can you name the patron saint of England?

**checklist** – Religion

Now you have read Section 3, can you remember the following?

■ **The percentage of the UK population who say they are Christian.**

■ **How many people say they have no religion.**

■ What percentage of people are Muslim, Hindu, Sikh, Jewish, Buddhist.

■ That everyone in the UK has the right to practise their religion.

■ That the Anglican Church, or Church of England, is the church of the state in England (established church).

■ That the monarch (king or queen) is head of the Church of England.

■ That, in Scotland, the established church is the Presbyterian Church of Scotland. In Wales and Northern Ireland there is no established church.

■ The number of bank holidays.

■ The names of the patron saints for each country and when the patron saints' days occur in the four countries of the UK.

■ That there are four bank holidays and four public holidays in England and Wales.

# SECTION 4 Customs and traditions

In this section you will read about:

■ the main festivals and traditions that are celebrated in the UK;

■ the role sport plays in people's lives and some of the main sporting events.

## Festivals

Throughout the year there are festivals of art, music and culture, such as the Notting Hill Carnival in west London and the Edinburgh Festival. Customs and traditions from various religions, such as Eid-ul-Fitr (Muslim), Diwali (Hindu) and Hanukkah (Jewish) are widely recognised in the UK. Children learn about these at school. The main Christian festivals are Christmas and Easter. There are also celebrations of non-religious traditions, such as New Year.

**The main Christian festivals**
**Christmas Day**
25 December celebrates the birth of Jesus Christ. It is a public holiday. Many Christians go to church on Christmas Eve (24 December) or on Christmas Day itself. Christmas is also usually celebrated by people who are not Christian. People usually spend the day at home and eat a special meal, which often includes turkey. They give each other gifts, send each other cards and decorate their houses. Many people decorate a tree. Christmas is a special time for children. Very young children believe that an old man, Father Christmas (or Santa Claus), brings them presents during the night. He is always shown in pictures with a long white beard, dressed in red. Boxing Day, 26 December, is the day after Christmas. It is a public holiday.

## Easter

Easter is the festival that marks for Christians when they believe Jesus Christ rose from the dead. The date of Easter changes each year but it is always a Sunday in March or April. There are two public holidays associated with it – Good Friday and Easter Monday. There are some special Easter customs, such as Easter eggs, that are not Christian in origin.

HELPING YOU LEARN

**3.14**   Can you name the TWO main Christian festivals?
**3.15**   Is the following statement TRUE or FALSE?
         26 December is not a public holiday.

# Other festivals and traditions

### New Year
1 January is a public holiday. People usually celebrate on the night of 31 December. In Scotland, 31 December is called Hogmanay and 2 January is also a public holiday. In Scotland Hogmanay is a bigger holiday for some people than Christmas.

### St Valentine's Day
14 February is when lovers exchange cards and gifts. Sometimes people send anonymous cards to someone they secretly admire.

### April Fool's Day
1 April is a day when people play jokes on each other until midday. Often TV and newspapers carry stories intended to deceive credulous viewers and readers.

### Mother's Day
The Sunday three weeks before Easter is a day when children send cards or buy gifts for their mothers. Easter is also an important Christian festival.

### Hallowe'en
31 October is a very ancient festival. Young people will often dress up in frightening costumes to play 'trick or treat'. Giving them sweets or chocolates might stop them playing a trick on you. Sometimes people carry lanterns made out of pumpkins with a candle inside.

### Guy Fawkes Night
5 November is an occasion when people in Great Britain set off fireworks at home or in special displays. The origin of the celebration was an event in 1605, when a group of Catholics led by Guy Fawkes failed in their plan to kill the Protestant king with a bomb in the Houses of Parliament.

### Remembrance Day
11 November commemorates those who died fighting in World War 1, World War 2 and other wars. Many people wear poppies (a red flower) in memory of those who died. At 11 a.m. there is a two-minute silence.

---

STUDY TIP

To help you remember the dates in this section, why not make a timeline from 1 January to 31 December?

Look back to Chapter 2, Figure 2.2 (page 27) if you need help doing this.

You might find it helpful to imagine a picture of an event and include the date in the picture, for example, a heart with the number 14 on to help you remember St Valentine's Day is on 14 February.

Another example could be an explosion of fireworks on 5 November, Guy Fawkes night.

---

HELPING YOU LEARN

**3.16**   Look at the list below and choose which flower many people wear on Remembrance Day in memory of those who died in the wars.

**A**. Tulip          **B**. Rose          **C**. Poppy

**3.17**   What is 31 December called in Scotland?

**Figure 3.9**
Hallowe'en is on 31 October, when young people often dress up and play 'trick or treat'.

## Sport

Sport of all kinds plays an important part in many people's lives. Football, tennis, rugby and cricket are very popular sports in the UK. There are no United Kingdom teams for football and rugby. England, Scotland, Wales and Northern Ireland have their own teams. Important sporting events include the Grand National horse race, the Football Association (FA) cup final (and equivalents in Northern Ireland, Scotland and Wales), the Open golf championship and the Wimbledon tennis tournament.

**Figure 3.10**
Cricket is popular in the UK.

## HELPING YOU LEARN

**3.18** Which sport is played at Wimbledon?

**checklist** – Customs and traditions

Now you have read Section 4, can you remember the following?

■ That the main festivals in the UK are Christian-based, but that important festivals from other religions are recognised and explained to children in schools.

■ When Christmas occurs and how it is celebrated.

■ The main traditional festivals in the UK and their dates.

■ That, in Scotland, the public holidays are different from those in England and Wales.

■ Popular sports in the UK and the main sporting events.

# SECTION 5  Revision questions and end of chapter checklist

Now you have finished reading the official study material, try to answer the following questions to see how much of Chapter 3 you can remember. If you are unsure of the answers, check your notes and refer back to the text before looking at the answers at the end of the book.

## Revision questions for Chapter 3

1. Is the Geordie dialect spoken in Liverpool?

Answer_____

2. Which country is St Andrew the patron saint of?

Answer_____

3. When is St Valentine's Day?

Answer_____

4. When will the next census be taken?

Answer_____

5. In which city is the Notting Hill carnival held?

Answer_____

6. What is the Grand National?

Answer_____

7. When is Hogmanay celebrated?

Answer_____

8. What percentage of the population of the UK live in England?

Answer_____

9. Who is the spiritual leader of the Church of England?

Answer_____

10. What percentage of the population attend religious services in the UK?

Answer_____

---

### End of Chapter 3 checklist

Now that you have come to the end of Chapter 3, tick the boxes when you have:

- read the study material; ☐
- made short notes to help you with your revision; ☐
- made a note of any words that you do not understand; ☐
- completed the *Helping you learn* and revision questions and checked your answers; ☐
- gone back and read again the sections for the questions you got wrong. ☐

Well done, you have now finished Chapter 3 of the study material and are ready to move on to Chapter 4.

## Answers to *Helping you learn* questions for Chapter 3

| | | |
|---|---|---|
| 3.1 | England | 50.1 million |
| | Scotland | 5.1 million |
| | Wales | 2.9 million |
| | Northern Ireland | 1.7 million |
| 3.2 | A | |
| 3.3 | Occupation | |
| | Ethnicity | |
| 3.4 | True | |
| 3.5 | London | |
| | West Midlands | |
| | South East | |
| | North West | |
| | Yorkshire and Humberside | |
| 3.6 | Scotland | 2% |
| | Northern Ireland | Less than 1% |
| | England | 9% |
| | Wales | 2% |
| 3.7 | 45% | |
| 3.8 | Scotland | Gaelic |
| | Northern Ireland | Irish Gaelic |
| | Wales | Welsh |
| | Liverpool | Scouse |
| | Tyneside | Geordie |
| | London | Cockney |
| 3.9 | 10% | |
| 3.10 | True | |
| 3.11 | Archbishop of Canterbury | |
| 3.12 | B and D | |
| 3.13 | St George | |
| 3.14 | Christmas and Easter | |
| 3.15 | False | |
| 3.16 | C | |
| 3.17 | Hogmanay | |
| 3.18 | Tennis | |

# CHAPTER 4

# How the United Kingdom is governed

In this chapter you will read about the system of government in the UK. You will learn about the roles of the monarchy and government, the political parties and the electoral system. There is also information about the voting system and the devolved parliaments for Wales, Scotland and Northern Ireland.

You will also read about the roles of the Commonwealth, the European Union and the United Nations.

To make it easier for you to learn, the information in this chapter is divided into three sections.

**Section 1** The British Constitution.

**Section 2** The UK in Europe and the world.

**Section 3** Revision questions and end of chapter checklist.

## SECTION 1 The British Constitution

In this section you will read about:

■ the system of government;

■ the monarchy;

■ the electoral system;

- **political parties;**
- **being a citizen;**
- **voting;**
- **how to contact your MP.**

## The British Constitution

As a constitutional democracy, the United Kingdom is governed by a wide range of institutions, many of which provide checks on each other's powers. Most of these institutions are of long standing: they include the monarchy, Parliament (consisting of the House of Commons and the House of Lords), the office of Prime Minister, the Cabinet, the judiciary, the police, the civil service, and the institutions of local government. More recently, devolved administrations have been set up for Scotland, Wales and Northern Ireland. Together, these formal institutions, laws and conventions form the British Constitution. Some people would argue that the roles of other less formal institutions, such as the media and pressure groups, should also be seen as part of the Constitution.

The British Constitution is not written down in any single document as are the constitutions of many other countries. This is mainly because the United Kingdom has never had a lasting revolution, like America or France, so our most important institutions have been in existence for hundreds of years. Some people believe that there should be a single document, but others believe that an unwritten constitution allows more scope for institutions to adapt to meet changing circumstances and public expectations.

**Figure 4.1**
The Houses of Parliament.

---

STUDY TIP

Using the information in Figure 4.2, why not try making a spider diagram to help you remember the structure of the British Constitution?

If you are not sure what a spider diagram looks like, there is an example in Chapter 1 (page 20).

---

# The monarchy

Queen Elizabeth II is the Head of State of the United Kingdom. She is also the monarch or Head of State for many countries in the Commonwealth. The UK, like Denmark, the Netherlands, Norway, Spain and Sweden, has a constitutional monarchy. This means that the king or queen does not rule the country, but appoints the government which the people have chosen in democratic elections. Although the queen or king can advise, warn and encourage the Prime Minister, the decisions on government policies are made by the Prime Minister and Cabinet.

The Queen has reigned since her father's death in 1952. Prince Charles, the Prince of Wales, her oldest son, is the heir to the throne.

The Queen has important ceremonial roles, such as the opening of the new parliamentary session each year. On this occasion the Queen makes a speech that summarises the government's policies for the year ahead.

**Figure 4.2**

> **The British Constitution consists of:**
>
> The Monarchy
>
> Parliament
>     House of Commons
>     House of Lords
>
> Prime Minister
> Cabinet
> Judiciary
> Police
> Civil service
> Local government
>
> Devolved administrations
>     Welsh Assembly
>     Northern Ireland Assembly
>     Parliament of Scotland

### HELPING YOU LEARN

**4.1**  Does the Queen make decisions on government policies?

**4.2**  Can you remember who the Head of State is in the UK?

**4.3**  Which of these statements is correct?
  **A**. Prince William is the heir to the throne.
  **B**. Prince Charles is the heir to the throne.

When you have completed these questions, you can check your answers at the end of the chapter.

## Government

The system of government in the United Kingdom is a parliamentary democracy. The UK is divided into 646 parliamentary constituencies and at least every five years voters in each constituency elect their Member of Parliament (MP) in a general election. All of the elected MPs form the House of Commons. Most MPs belong to a political party and the party with the largest number of MPs forms the government.

The law that requires new elections to Parliament to be held at least every five years is so fundamental that no government has sought to change it. A Bill to change it is the only one to which the House of Lords must give its consent.

Some people argue that the power of Parliament is lessened because of the obligation of the United Kingdom to accept the rules of the European Union and the judgements of the European Court, but it was Parliament itself which created these obligations.

### DID YOU KNOW?

**Did you know that it is a tradition that the House of Lords has red leather benches and carpets, and that the House of Commons has green leather benches and carpets?**

### HELPING YOU LEARN

**4.4**  How many parliamentary constituencies is the UK divided into?

# The House of Commons

The House of Commons is the more important of the two chambers in Parliament, and its members are democratically elected. Nowadays the Prime Minster and almost all the members of the Cabinet are members of the House of Commons. The members of the House of Commons are called 'Members of Parliament' or MPs for short. Each MP represents a parliamentary constituency, or area of the country: there are 646 of these. MPs have a number of different responsibilities. They represent everyone in their constituency, they help to create new laws, they scrutinise and comment on what the government is doing, and they debate important national issues.

### Elections

There must be a general election to elect MPs at least every five years, though they may be held sooner if the Prime Minister so decides. If an MP dies or resigns, there will be another election, called a by-election, in his or her constituency. MPs are elected through a system called 'first past the post'. In each constituency, the candidate who gets the most votes is elected. The government is then formed by the party which won the majority of constituencies.

HELPING YOU LEARN

**4.5**   Without looking at the text, can you remember how often the law requires new elections to Parliament to be held?

**4.6**   Is the following statement TRUE or FALSE?
The more important of the two Parliament chambers is the House of Lords.

# The Whips

The Whips are a small group of MPs appointed by their party leaders. They are responsible for discipline in their party and making sure MPs attend the House of Commons to vote. The Chief Whip often attends Cabinet or Shadow Cabinet meetings and arranges the schedule of proceedings in the House of Commons with the speaker.

**4.7**   Who are the Whips appointed by?

**Figure 4.3** The House of Commons in session.

# European parliamentary elections

Elections for the European Parliament are also held every five years.
There are 78 seats for representatives from the UK in the European
Parliament and elected members are called Members of the European
Parliament (MEPs). Elections to the European Parliament use a system of
proportional representation, whereby seats are allocated to each party in
proportion to the total votes it won.

**4.8**   How often are elections held for the European Parliament?

# The House of Lords

Members of the House of Lords, known as peers, are not elected and do not represent a constituency. The role and membership of the House of Lords have recently undergone big changes. Until 1958 all peers were either 'hereditary', meaning that their titles were inherited, senior judges, or bishops of the Church of England. Since 1958 the Prime Minister has had the power to appoint peers just for their own lifetime. These peers, known as Life Peers, have usually had a distinguished career in politics, business, law or some other profession. This means that debates in the House of Lords often draw on more specialist knowledge than is available to members of the House of Commons. Life Peers are appointed by the Queen on the advice of the Prime Minister, but they include people nominated by the leaders of the other main parties and by an independent Appointments Commission for non-party peers.

In the last few years the hereditary peers have lost the automatic right to attend the House of Lords, although they are allowed to elect a few of their number to represent them.

While the House of Lords is usually the less important of the two chambers of Parliament, it is more independent of government. It can suggest amendments or propose new laws, which are then discussed by the House of Commons. The House of Lords can become very important if the majority of its members will not agree to pass a law for which the House of Commons has voted. The House of Commons has powers to overrule the House of Lords, but these are very rarely used.

HELPING YOU LEARN

**4.9**   Who of the following appoints Life Peers?
   **A**.  The Queen
   **B**.  The Prime Minister
   **C**.  The Whips
   **D**.  Leader of the Opposition

**4.10**  Which of these statements is correct?
   **A**.  Life Peers were first introduced in 1938.
   **B**.  Life Peers were first introduced in 1958.

# The Prime Minister

The Prime Minister (PM) is the leader of the political party in power. He or she appoints the members of the Cabinet and has control over many important public appointments. The official home of the Prime Minister is 10 Downing Street, in central London, near the Houses of Parliament; he or she also has a country house not far from London called Chequers. The Prime Minister can be changed if the MPs in the governing party decide to do so, or if he or she wishes to resign. More usually, the Prime Minister resigns when his or her party is defeated in a general election.

**The Cabinet**
The Prime Minster appoints about 20 senior MPs to become ministers in charge of departments. These include the Chancellor of the Exchequer, responsible for the economy, the Home Secretary, responsible for law, order and immigration, the Foreign Secretary, and ministers (called 'Secretaries of State') for education, health and defence. The Lord Chancellor, who is the minister responsible for legal affairs, is also a member of the Cabinet but sat in the House of Lords rather than the House of Commons. Following legislation passed in 2005, it is now possible for the Lord Chancellor to sit in the Commons. These ministers form the Cabinet, a small committee which usually meets weekly and makes important decisions about government policy. These decisions often then have to be debated or approved by Parliament.

---

DID YOU KNOW?

Did you know that the first person to be Prime Minister was Sir Robert Walpole? He was Prime Minister for 20 years.

---

HELPING YOU LEARN

**4.11** Where is the official home of the Prime Minister?

**4.12** Look at Figure 4.4 and try to add one further member of the cabinet. Choose one from the following:

Whip          Chancellor of the Exchequer

Figure 4.4

**Members of the cabinet**

Prime Minister

................................

Foreign Secretary

Lord Chancellor

## The Opposition

The second largest party in the House of Commons is called the Opposition. The Leader of the Opposition is the person who hopes to become Prime Minister if his or her party wins the next general election. The Leader of the Opposition leads his or her party in pointing out the government's failures and weaknesses; one important opportunity to do this is at Prime Minister's Questions, which takes place every week while Parliament is sitting. The Leader of the Opposition also appoints senior Opposition MPs to lead the criticism of government ministers, and together they form the Shadow Cabinet.

**The Speaker**

Debates in the House of Commons are chaired by the Speaker, the chief officer of the House of Commons. The Speaker is politically neutral. He or she is an MP, elected by fellow MPs to keep order during political debates and to make sure the rules are followed. This includes making sure the Opposition has a guaranteed amount of time to debate issues it chooses. The Speaker also represents Parliament at ceremonial occasions.

HELPING YOU LEARN

**4.13**  Can you remember how often Prime Minister's Questions takes place?

# The party system

Under the British system of parliamentary democracy, anyone can stand for election as an MP but they are unlikely to win an election unless they have been nominated to represent one of the major political parties. These are the Labour Party, the Conservative Party, the Liberal Democrats, or one of the parties representing Scottish, Welsh, or Northern Irish interests. There are just a few MPs who do not represent any of the main political parties and are called 'independents'. The main political parties actively seek members among ordinary voters to join their debates, contribute to their costs, and help at elections for Parliament or for local government; they have branches in most constituencies and they hold policy-making conferences every year.

---

H E L P I N G   Y O U   L E A R N

**4.14** Can you name the three major political parties?

**4.15** Look at the list below in Figure 4.5 and match up the roles to the correct definitions. One has been done for you as an example. If you are unsure, use the study material to help you. You may want to use this to help you with your revision later.

---

**British Parliamentary system**

1. Whips                              **A.** Appointed by the Queen on the advice of the Prime Minister.

2. Prime Minister                     **B.** A small committee of ministers that make important decisions about government policy.

3. Life Peers                         **C.** Small group of MPs appointed by party leaders responsible for discipline in their party.

4. MPs                                **D.** Leader of the political party in power.

5. Leader of the Opposition           **E.** Members of Parliament.

6. Members of the cabinet.            **F.** The person who leads their party and points out the government's failures and weaknesses.

**Figure 4.5**

HELPING YOU LEARN

**4.16** Now look at Figure 4.6 and decide in which of the Houses of Parliament the following government roles belong. An example has been done for you.
1. MPs
2. Life Peers
3. Hereditary peers
4. Prime Minister
5. Whips
6. Senior bishops and judges
7. Members of the Opposition
8. Leader of the Opposition
9. Members of the Cabinet

**Figure 4.6**

| House of Lords | House of Commons | |
|---|---|---|
| ........................... | Prime Minister | |
| ........................... | ........................... | ........................... |
| ........................... | ........................... | ........................... |
| | ........................... | ........................... |

# Pressure and lobby groups

Pressure and lobby groups are organisations that try to influence government policy. They play a very important role in politics. There are many pressure groups in the UK. They may represent economic interests (such as the Confederation of British Industry, the Consumers' Association, or the trade unions) or views on particular subjects (e.g. Greenpeace or Liberty). The general public is more likely to support pressure groups than join a political party.

## The civil service

Civil servants are managers and administrators who carry out government policy. They have to be politically neutral and professional, regardless of which political party is in power. Although civil servants have to follow the policies of the elected government, they can warn ministers if they think a policy is impractical or not in the public interest. Before a general election takes place, top level servants study the Opposition party's policies closely in case they need to be ready to serve a new government with different aims and policies.

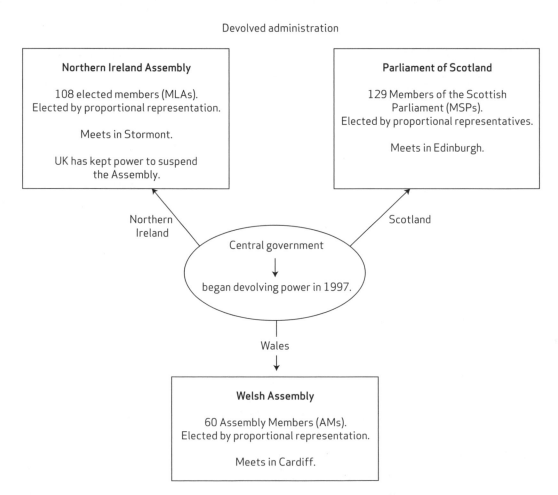

Devolved administration

**Northern Ireland Assembly**

108 elected members (MLAs).
Elected by proportional representation.

Meets in Stormont.

UK has kept power to suspend the Assembly.

**Parliament of Scotland**

129 Members of the Scottish Parliament (MSPs).
Elected by proportional representatives.

Meets in Edinburgh.

Northern Ireland

Scotland

Central government
↓
began devolving power in 1997.

Wales
↓

**Welsh Assembly**

60 Assembly Members (AMs).
Elected by proportional representation.

Meets in Cardiff.

**Figure 4.7** Diagram to help you remember information about devolved administrations.

# Devolved administration

In order to give people in Wales and Scotland more control of matters that directly affect them, in 1997 the government began a programme of devolving power from central government. Since 1999 there has been a Welsh Assembly, a Scottish Parliament and, periodically, a Northern Ireland Assembly. Although policy and laws governing defence, foreign affairs, taxation and social security all remain under central UK government control, many other public services now come under the control of the devolved administrations in Wales and Scotland.

Both the Scottish Parliament and Welsh Assembly have been set up using forms of proportional representation, which ensures that each party gets a number of seats in proportion to the number of votes they receive. Similarly, proportional representation is used in Northern Ireland in order to ensure 'power sharing' between the Unionist majority (mainly Protestant) and the substantial (mainly Catholic) minority aligned to Irish nationalist parties. A different form of proportional representation is used for elections to the European Parliament.

# The Welsh Assembly Government

The National Assembly for Wales, or Welsh Assembly Government (WAG), is situated in Cardiff, the capital city of Wales. It has 60 Assembly Members (AMs) and elections are held every four years. Members can speak in either Welsh or English and all its publications are in both languages. The Assembly has the power to make decisions on important matters such as education policy, the environment, health services, transport and local government, and to pass laws for Wales on these matters within a statutory framework set out by the UK Parliament at Westminster.

**4.17** Can you remember in which year the government began a programme of devolving government from central government?

**4.18** In which city is the National Assembly for Wales situated? If you need help look back at Figure 4.7.

# The Parliament of Scotland

A long campaign in Scotland for more independence and democratic control led to the formation in 1999 of the Parliament of Scotland, which sits in Edinburgh, the capital of Scotland.

There are 129 Members of the Scottish Parliament (MSPs), elected by a form of proportional representation. This has led to the sharing of power in Scotland between the Labour and Liberal Democrat parties. The Scottish Parliament can pass legislation for Scotland on all matters that are not specifically reserved to the UK Parliament. The matters on which the Scottish Parliament can legislate include civil and criminal law, health, education, planning and the raising of additional taxes.

**4.19** How many Members of the Scottish Parliament (MSPs) are there?
   **A**. 181
   **B**. 129
   **C**. 152
   **D**. 138

# The Northern Ireland Assembly

A Northern Ireland Parliament was established in 1922 when Ireland was divided, but it was abolished in 1972 shortly after the Troubles broke out in 1969.

Soon after the end of the Troubles, the Northern Ireland Assembly was established with a power-sharing agreement which distributes ministerial offices among the main parties. The Assembly has 108 elected members known as MLAs (Members of the Legislative Assembly). Decision-making powers devolved to Northern Ireland include education, agriculture, the environment, health and social services in Northern Ireland.

The UK government kept the power to suspend the Northern Ireland Assembly if the political leaders no longer agreed to work together or if the Assembly was not working in the interests of the people of Northern Ireland. This has happened several times and the Assembly is currently suspended (2006). This means that the elected Assembly Members do not have power to pass bills or make decisions.

## HELPING YOU LEARN

**4.20** Is the following statement TRUE or FALSE?
The UK Government has the power to suspend the Northern Ireland Assembly.

# Local government

Towns, cities and rural areas in the UK are governed by democratically elected councils, often called local authorities. Some areas have both district and county councils, which have different functions, although most larger towns and cities will have a single local authority. Many councils representing towns and cities appoint a mayor, who is the ceremonial leader of the council, but in some towns a mayor is appointed to be the effective leader of the administration. London has

33 local authorities, with the Greater London Authority and the Mayor of London co-ordinating policies across the capital. Local authorities are required to provide 'mandatory services' in their area. These services include education, housing, social services, passenger transport, the fire service, rubbish collection, planning, environmental health and libraries.

Most of the money for the local authority services comes from the government through taxes. Only about 20% is funded locally through 'council tax' – a local tax set by councils to help pay for local services. It applies to all domestic properties, including houses, bungalows, flats, maisonettes, mobile homes or houseboats, whether owned or rented.

Local elections for councillors are held in May every year. Many candidates stand for council election as members of a political party.

## HELPING YOU LEARN

**4.21** Which of the following statements is correct?

   **A.**   Most of the money for local authority services comes from the government through taxes.

   **B.**   Most of the money for local authority services comes from council tax.

# The judiciary

In the UK the laws made by Parliament are the highest authority. But often important questions arise about how the laws are to be interpreted in particular cases. It is the task of the judges (who are together called 'the judiciary') to interpret the law, and the government may not interfere with their role. Often the actions of the government are claimed to be illegal and, if the judges agree, then the government must either change its policies or ask Parliament to change the law. This has become all the more important in recent years, as the judges now have the task of applying the Human Rights Act. If they find that a public body is not respecting a person's human rights, they may order the body to change its practices and to pay compensation, if appropriate. If the judges believe that an Act of Parliament is incompatible with the Human Rights Act, they cannot change it themselves but they can ask Parliament to consider doing so.

Judges cannot, however, decide whether people are guilty or innocent of serious crimes. When someone is accused of a serious crime, a jury will decide whether he or she is innocent or guilty and, if guilty, the judge will decide on the penalty. For less important crimes, a magistrate will decide on guilt and on any penalty.

HELPING YOU LEARN

**4.22**  Which of the following statements is correct?
  **A**.  When someone is accused of a serious crime the jury decides if the person is guilty or innocent.
  **B**.  When someone is accused of a serious crime the judge decides if the person is guilty or innocent.

# The police

The police service is organised locally, with one police service for each county or group of counties. The largest force is the Metropolitan Police, which serves London and is based at New Scotland Yard. Northern Ireland as a whole is served by the Police Service for Northern Ireland (PSNI). The police have 'operational independence', which means that the government cannot instruct them on what to do in any particular case. But the powers of the police are limited by the law and their finances are controlled by the government and by police authorities made up of councillors and magistrates. The Independent Police Complaints Commission (or, in Northern Ireland, the Police Ombudsman) investigates serious complaints against the police.

## Non-departmental public bodies (quangos)

Non-departmental public bodies, also known as quangos, are independent organisations that carry out functions on behalf of the public which it would be inappropriate to place under the political control of a Cabinet minister. There are many hundreds of these bodies, carrying out a wide variety of public duties. Appointments to these bodies are usually made by ministers, but they must do so in an open and fair way.

## The role of the media

Proceedings in Parliament are broadcast on digital television and published in official reports such as Hansard, which is available in large libraries and on the internet: **www.parliament.uk**. Most people, however, get information about political issues and events from newspapers (often called the press), television and radio.

The UK has a free press, meaning that what is written in newspapers is free from government control. Newspaper owners and editors hold strong political opinions and run campaigns to try to influence government policy and public opinion. As a result, it is sometimes difficult to distinguish fact from opinion in newspaper coverage.

By law, radio and television coverage of the political parties at election periods must be balanced and so equal time has to be given to rival viewpoints. But broadcasters are free to interview politicians in a tough and lively way.

HELPING YOU LEARN

**4.23** Is the following statement TRUE or FALSE?
The government controls what is written in newspapers.

# Who can vote?

The United Kingdom has had a fully democratic system since 1928, when women were allowed to vote at 21, the same age as men. The present voting age of 18 was set in 1969, and (with a few exceptions such as convicted prisoners) all UK-born and naturalised citizens have full civic rights, including the right to vote and do jury service.

Citizens of the UK, the Commonwealth and the Irish Republic (if resident in the UK) can vote in all public elections. Citizens of EU states who are resident in the UK can vote in all elections except national parliamentary (general) elections.

In order to vote in a parliamentary, local or European election, you must have your name on the register of electors, known as the electoral register. If you are eligible to vote, you can register by contacting your local council election registration office. If you don't know what your local authority is, you can find out by telephoning the Local Government Association (LGA) information line on 0207 664 3131 between 9 a.m. and 5 p.m., Monday to Friday. You will have to tell them your postcode or your full address and they will be able to give you the name of your local authority. You can also get voter registration forms in English, Welsh and some other languages on the internet: **www.electoralcommission.org.uk**.

The electoral register is updated every year in September or October. An electoral registration form is sent to every household and it has to be completed and returned, with the names of everyone who is resident in the household and eligible to vote on 15 October.

In Northern Ireland a different system operates. This is called individual registration and all those entitled to vote must complete their own registration form. Once registered, you can stay on the register provided your personal details do not change. For more information, telephone the Electoral Office for Northern Ireland on 028 9044 6688.

By law, each local authority has to make its electoral register available for anyone to look at, although this now has to be supervised. The register is kept at each local electoral registration office (or council office in England and Wales). It is also possible to see the register at some public buildings such as libraries.

HELPING YOU LEARN

**4.24**   In the UK how old do you have to be to vote?

## Standing for office

Most citizens of the United Kingdom, the Irish Republic or the Commonwealth aged 18 or over can stand for public office. There are some exceptions and these include members of the armed forces, civil servants and people found guilty of certain criminal offences. Members of the House of Lords may not stand for election to the House of Commons but are eligible for all other public offices.

To become a local councillor, a candidate must have a local connection with the area through work, being on the electoral register, or through renting or owning land or property.

## Contacting elected members

All elected members have a duty to serve and represent their constituents. You can get contact details for all your representatives and their parties from your local library. Assembly Members, MSPs, MPs and MEPs are also listed in the phone book and Yellow Pages. You can contact MPs by letter or phone at their constituency office or their office in the House of Commons: The House of Commons, Westminster, London, SW1A 0AA or telephone: 0207 729 3000. Many Assembly Members, MSPs, MPs and MEPs hold regular local 'surgeries'. These are often advertised in the local paper and constituents can go and talk about issues in person. You can find out the name of your local MP and get in touch with them by fax through the website: **www.writetothem.com**. This service is free.

**4.25**  Is the following statement TRUE or FALSE?
Members of the armed forces are allowed to stand for public office.

# How to visit Parliament and devolved administrations

■ The public can listen to debates in the Palace of Westminster from public galleries in both the House of Commons and the House of Lords. You can either write to your local MP in advance to ask for tickets or you can queue on the day at the public entrance. Entrance is free. Sometimes there are long queues for the House of Commons and you may have to wait for at least one or two hours. It is usually easier to get into the House of Lords. You can find further information on the UK Parliament website: **www.parliament.uk**.

■ In Northern Ireland, elected members, known as MLAs, meet in the Northern Ireland Assembly at Stormont, in Belfast. The Northern Ireland Assembly is presently suspended. There are two ways to arrange a visit to Stormont. You can either contact the Education Service (details on the Northern Ireland Assembly website: **www.niassembly.gov.uk**) or contact an MLA.

■ In Scotland, the elected members, called MSPs, meet in the Scottish Parliament at Holyrood in Edinburgh (for more information see: **www.scottish.parliament.uk**). You can get information, book tickets or arrange tours through the visitor services. You can write to them at The Scottish Parliament, Edinburgh, EH99 1SP, or telephone 0131 348 5200, or email **sp.bookings@scottish.parliament.uk**.

■ In Wales, the elected members, known as AMs, meet in the Welsh Assembly in the Seneff Cardiff Bay (for more information see: **www.wales.gov.uk**). You can book guided tours or seats in the public galleries for the Welsh Assembly. To make a booking, telephone the Assembly booking line on 029 2089 8477 or email: **assembly.booking@wales.gsi.gov.uk**.

HELPING YOU LEARN

**4.26**  Is the following statement TRUE or FALSE?
The public can listen to debates in the Palace of Westminster but you must buy a ticket in advance.

**checklist** – The British Constitution

Now you have read Section 1, can you remember the following?

■ The role of the monarchy.

■ How Parliament works, and the difference between the House of Commons and the House of Lords.

■ How often general elections are held.

■ Where the official residence of the Prime Minister is.

■ The role of the Cabinet and who is in it.

■ The nature of the UK Constitution.

■ The job of the Opposition, the Leader of the Opposition and the Shadow Cabinet.

■ The difference between 'first past the post' and proportional representation.

■ The form of electoral systems in the devolved administrations of Northern Ireland, Scotland and Wales.

■ The rights and duties of British citizens, including naturalised citizens.

■ How the judiciary, police and local authorities work.

■ What non-departmental public bodies are.

# SECTION 2 The UK in Europe and the world

In this section you will read about:

■ the European Union;

■ the Commonwealth;

■ the United Nations.

## The Commonwealth

The Commonwealth is an association of countries, most of which were once part of the British Empire, although a few countries that were not in the Empire have also joined it.

**Commonwealth members** (list continues on page 92)

| | |
|---|---|
| Antigua and Barbuda | Malaysia |
| Australia | Maldives |
| The Bahamas | Malta |
| Bangladesh | Mauritius |
| Barbados | Mozambique |
| Belize | Namibia |
| Botswana | Nauru* |
| Brunei Darussalam | New Zealand |
| Cameroon | Nigeria |
| Canada | Pakistan |
| Cyprus | Papua New Guinea |
| Dominica | St Kitts and Nevis |
| Fiji Islands | St Lucia |
| The Gambia | St Vincent and the Grenadines |
| Ghana | Samoa |
| Grenada | Seychelles |
| Guyana | Sierra Leone |
| India | Singapore |
| Jamaica | Solomon Islands |
| Kenya | South Africa |
| Kiribati | Sri Lanka |
| Lesotho | Swaziland |
| Malawi | Tonga |

| | |
|---|---|
| Trinidad and Tobago | United Republic of Tanzania |
| Tuvalu | Vanuatu |
| Uganda | Zambia |
| United Kingdom | |

* Nauru is a Special Member

The Queen is the head of the Commonwealth, which currently has 53 member states. Membership is voluntary and the Commonwealth has no power over its members although it can suspend membership. The Commonwealth aims to promote democracy and good government and to eradicate poverty.

### HELPING YOU LEARN

**4.27** Who is the head of the Commonwealth?

**4.28** How many countries are in the Commonwealth?

**Figure 4.8** The Queen at the Commonwealth Heads of Government conference (Photo: Roberto Schmidt/AFP/Getty Images)

# The European Union (EU)

The European Union (EU), originally called the European Economic Community (EEC), was set up by six Western European countries who signed the Treaty of Rome on 25 March 1957. One of the main reasons for doing this was the belief that co-operation between states would reduce the likelihood of another war in Europe. Originally the UK decided not to join this group and only became part of the European Union in 1973. In 2004 ten new member countries joined the EU, with a further two in 2006, making a total of 27 member countries.

One of the main aims of the EU today is for member states to function as a single market. Most of the countries of the EU have a shared currency, the euro, but the UK has decided to retain its own currency unless the British people choose to accept the euro in a referendum. Citizens of an EU member state have the right to travel to and work in any EU country if they have a valid passport or identity card. This right can be restricted on the grounds of public health, public order and public security. The right to work is also sometimes restricted for citizens of countries that have joined the EU recently.

The Council of the European Union (usually called the Council of Ministers) is effectively the governing body of the EU. It is made up of government ministers from each country in the EU and, together with the European Parliament, is the legislative body of the EU. The Council of Ministers passes EU law on the recommendations of the European Commission and the European Parliament, and takes the most important decisions about how the EU is run. The European Commission is based in Brussels, the capital city of Belgium. It is the civil service of the EU and drafts proposals for new EU policies and laws, and administers its funding programmes.

The European Parliament meets in Strasbourg, in north-eastern France, and in Brussels. Each country elects members, called Members of the European Parliament (MEPs), every five years. The European Parliament examines decisions made by the European Council and the European Commission, and it has the power to refuse agreement to European laws proposed by the Commission and to check on the spending of EU funds.

European Union law is legally binding in the UK and all the other member states. European laws, called directives, regulations or framework decisions, have made a lot of difference to people's rights in the UK, particularly at work. For example, there are EU directives about the procedures for making workers redundant, and regulations that limit the number of hours people can be made to work.

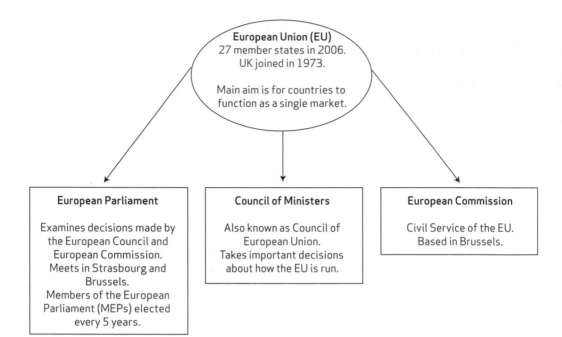

**Figure 4.9** The structure of the European Union.

---

IMPORTANT INFORMATION

You may find the following European bodies confusing as they have similar names but they have different responsibilities.

■ The Council of the European Union (usually called the Council of Ministers) is part of the legislative body of the EU (see Figure 4.9).

■ The Council of Europe is a separate organisation and does not have powers to make laws. It draws up conventions and charters, for example the European Convention on Human Rights.

HELPING YOU LEARN

**4.29** Is the following statement TRUE or FALSE?
Most countries of the EU have a shared currency, the euro.

**4.30** In which TWO places does the European Parliament meet?
  **A**. London
  **B**. Paris
  **C**. Brussels
  **D**. Strasbourg

**Figure 4.10**   In 2004, ten new member countries joined the EU, and a further two joined in 2006, making a total of 27 member countries.

# The Council of Europe

The Council of Europe was created in 1949 and the UK was one of the founder members. Most of the countries of Europe are members. It has no power to make laws but draws up conventions and charters which focus on human rights, democracy, education, the environment, health and culture. The most important of these is the European Convention on Human Rights; all member states are bound by this Convention and a member state which persistently refuses to obey the Convention may be expelled from the Council of Europe.

# The United Nations (UN)

The UK is a member of the United Nations (UN), an international organisation to which over 190 countries now belong. The UN was set up after the Second World War and aims to prevent war and promote international peace and security. There are 15 members on the UN Security Council, which recommends action by the UN when there are international crises and threats to peace. The UK is one of the five permanent members.

Three very important agreements produced by the UN are the Universal Declaration of Human Rights, the Convention on the Elimination of All Forms of Discrimination against Women, and the UN Convention on the Rights of the Child. Although none of these has the force of law, they are widely used in political debate and legal cases to reinforce the law and to assess the behaviour of countries.

HELPING YOU LEARN

**4.31**  Is the following statement TRUE or FALSE?
The UK is a permanent member of the UN Security Council.

**4.32**  Which of the following is correct?
**A.**  The UN was set up after the First World War.
**B.**  The UN was set up after the Second World War.

checklist – The UK in Europe and the World

Now you have read Section 2, can you remember the following?

■ The differences between the Council of Europe, the European Union, the European Commission and the European Parliament.

■ That the UK is a member of the Council of Europe and the European Union.

■ That the EU aims to become a single market and that it is administered by a Council of Ministers of governments of member states.

■ That, subject to some restrictions, EU citizens may travel to and work in any EU country.

■ The roles of the UN and the Commonwealth.

# SECTION 3 Revision questions and end of chapter checklist

Now you have finished reading the official study material, try to answer the following questions to see how much of Chapter 4 you can remember. If you are unsure of the answers, check your notes and refer back to the text before looking at the answers at the end of the book.

## Revision questions for Chapter 4

1. What is the abbreviation PM short for?

Answer_____

2. Does the speaker of the House of Commons belong to a political party?

Answer_____

3. Does the UK have a written constitution?

Answer_____

4. Is Indonesia a member of the Commonwealth?

Answer_____

5. Does the monarch make decisions on government policies?

Answer_____

6. Can members of the public attend debates in the Houses of Parliament?

Answer_____

7. What is a quango?

Answer_____

8. What do the initials MEP stand for?

Answer_____

9. How many countries are in the European Union?

Answer_____

10. When was the Parliament of Scotland formed?

Answer_____

11. Are all members of both Houses of Parliament democratically elected?

Answer_____

12. Do you need to have your name on the electoral register to vote?

Answer_____

13. Does the government control what is written in the newspapers in the UK?

Answer_____

| **End of Chapter 4 checklist** |
| :--- |

Now that you have come to the end of Chapter 4, tick the boxes when you have:

■ read the study material;                                                      ☐

■ made short notes to help you with your revision;                              ☐

■ made a note and checked words that you do not
understand;                                                                      ☐

■ completed the *Helping you learn* and revision questions
and checked your answers;                                                        ☐

■ gone back and read again the sections for the
questions you got wrong.                                                         ☐

Well done, you have now finished Chapter 4 of the study material and are ready to move on to Chapter 5.

## Answers to *Helping you learn* questions for Chapter 4

4.1 No

4.2 The Queen

4.3 B

4.4 646

4.5 At least every five years

4.6 False

4.7 Party leaders

4.8 Every five years

4.9 A

4.10 B

4.11 10 Downing Street

4.12 Chancellor of the Exchequer

4.13 Once a week while Parliament is sitting

4.14 Conservative, Labour and Liberal Democrat

4.15 1 – C

2 – D

3 – A

4 – E

5 – F

6 – B

4.16   1 – House of Commons
      2 – House of Lords
      3 – House of Lords
      4 – House of Commons
      5 – House of Commons
      6 – House of Lords
      7 – House of Commons
      8 – House of Commons
      9 – House of Commons

4.17   1997

4.18   Cardiff

4.19   B

4.20   True

4.21   A

4.22   A

4.23   False – the UK has a free press

4.24   18

4.25   False

4.26   False – the public can listen to debates but you do not need to buy a ticket in advance

4.27   The Queen

4.28   53

4.29   True

4.30   C and D

4.31   True

4.32   B

# CHAPTER 5

# Everyday needs

In this chapter you will read about the main activities and services that are a part of everyday life in the UK. It includes information about buying or renting a home and arranging for services in the home, such as water, gas and electricity.

There is a section about banks and building societies with information on borrowing money and the use of credit and debit cards.

You will also read about the main government services, for example education and health, and the regional differences.

The chapter includes information about travel and transport, and popular leisure pursuits.

To make it easier for you to remember the information, the chapter is divided into eight sections.

**Section 1**  Housing.

**Section 2**  Services in and for the home.

**Section 3**  Money and credit.

**Section 4**  Health.

**Section 5**  Education.

**Section 6**  Leisure.

**Section 7**  Travel and transport.

**Section 8**  Revision questions and end of chapter checklist.

---

**STUDY TIP**

You will need to allow more time to read this chapter as it is the longest in the guide.

You may find it more manageable if you read it in small sections. To help you do this the chapter is already divided into easy stages.

Remember to take regular breaks and not to study for too long at a time.

---

# SECTION 1  Housing

In this section you will read about:

■ the process of buying and renting a home in the UK;

■ how to get help if you do not have a home.

**IMPORTANT** INFORMATION

If you have housing problems there is information and support in this chapter to help you.

**Figure 5.1**
An estate agent's sign outside a house for sale. (Photo by Matt Cardy/ Getty Images)

# Buying a home

Two-thirds of people in the UK own their own home. Most other people rent houses, flats or rooms.

## Mortgages

People who buy their own home usually pay for it with a mortgage, a special loan from a bank or building society. This loan is paid back, with interest, over a long period of time, usually 25 years. You can get information about mortgages from a bank or building society. Some banks can also give information about Islamic (Sharia) mortgages.

If you are having problems paying your mortgage repayments, you can get help and advice. It is important to speak to your bank or building society as soon as you can.

## Estate agents

If you wish to buy a home, usually the first place to start is an estate agent. In Scotland the process is different and you should go first to a solicitor. Estate agents represent the person selling their house or flat. They arrange for buyers to visit homes that are for sale. There are estate agents in all towns and cities, and they usually have websites where they advertise the homes for sale. You can also find details about homes for sale on the internet, and in national and local newspapers.

## Making an offer

In the UK, except in Scotland, when you find a home you wish to buy you have to make an offer to the seller. You usually do this through an estate agent or solicitor. Many people offer a lower price than the seller is asking. Your first offer must be 'subject to contract' so that you can withdraw if there are reasons why you cannot complete the purchase. In Scotland, the seller sets a price and buyers make offers over that amount. The agreement becomes legally binding earlier than it does elsewhere in the UK.

## Solicitor and surveyor

It is important that a solicitor helps you through the process of buying a house or flat. When you make an offer on a property, the solicitor will carry out a number of legal checks on the property, the seller and the local area. The solicitor will provide the legal agreements necessary for you to buy the property. The bank or building society that is providing you with your mortgage will also carry out checks on the house or flat you wish to buy. These are done by a surveyor. The buyer does not usually see the result of this survey, so the buyer often asks a second surveyor to check the house as well. In Scotland the survey is carried out before an offer is made, to help people decide how much they want to bid for the property.

## HELPING YOU LEARN

**5.1**   How do people who buy their own home usually pay for it?
**5.2**   Is the following statement TRUE or FALSE?
         A surveyor will provide the legal agreements for you to buy a property.

# Rented accommodation

It is possible to rent accommodation from the local authority (the council), from a housing association or from private property owners called landlords.

### The local authority

Most local authorities (or councils) provide housing. This is often called 'council housing'. In Northern Ireland social housing is provided by the Northern Ireland Housing Executive (**www.nihe.gov.uk**). In Scotland you can find information on social housing at: **www.sfha.co.uk**. Everyone is entitled to apply for council accommodation. To apply you must put your name on the council register or list. This is available from the housing department at the local authority. You are then assessed according to your needs. This is done through a system of points. You get more points if you have priority needs, for example if you are homeless and have children or chronic ill health.

It is important to note that in many areas of the UK there is a shortage of council accommodation, and that some people have to wait a very long time for a house or flat.

### Housing associations

Housing associations are independent not-for-profit organisations which provide housing for rent. In some areas they have taken over the administration of local authority housing. They also run schemes called shared ownership, which help people buy part of a house or flat if they cannot afford to buy all of it at once. There are usually waiting lists for homes owned by housing associations.

### Privately rented accommodation

Many people rent houses or flats privately, from landlords. Information about private accommodation can be found in local newspapers, notice boards, estate agents and letting agents.

---

HELPING YOU LEARN

**5.3** Which of the following statements is correct?
- **A.** The housing that local authorities provide is called council housing.
- **B.** The housing that local authorities provide is called private housing.

**5.4** Look at the text and see if you can name two organisations you can rent accommodation from.

---

# Tenancy agreement

When you rent a house or flat privately you sign a tenancy agreement, or lease. This explains the conditions or 'rules' you must follow while renting the property. This agreement must be checked very carefully to avoid problems later. The agreement also contains a list of any furniture or fittings in the property. This is called an inventory. Before you sign the agreement, check the details and keep it safe during your tenancy.

### Deposit and rent

You will probably be asked to give the landlord a deposit at the beginning of your tenancy. This is to cover the cost of any damage. It is usually equal to one month's rent. The landlord must return this money to you at the end of your tenancy, unless you have caused damage to the property.

Your rent is fixed with your landlord at the beginning of the tenancy. The landlord cannot raise the rent without your agreement.

If you have a low income or are unemployed you may be able to claim Housing Benefit to help you pay your rent.

### Renewing and ending a tenancy

Your tenancy agreement will be for a fixed period of time, often six months. After this time the tenancy can be ended or, if both tenant and landlord agree, renewed. If you end the tenancy before the fixed time, you usually have to pay the rent for the agreed full period of tenancy.

A landlord cannot force a tenant to leave. If a landlord wishes a tenant to leave they must follow the correct procedures. These vary according to the type of tenancy. It is a criminal offence for a landlord to use threats or violence against a tenant or to force them to leave without an order from court.

### Discrimination

It is unlawful for a landlord to discriminate against someone looking for accommodation because of their sex, race, nationality, or ethnic group, or because they are disabled, unless the landlord or a close relative of the landlord's is sharing the accommodation.

---

### HELPING YOU LEARN

**5.5** How much deposit would you normally give a landlord when you rent a property?

**5.6** Which of the following is the document that lists the furniture and fittings when you rent a property?
   **A**. Inventory
   **B**. Tenancy agreement

# Homelessness

If you are homeless you should go for help to the local authority (or, in Northern Ireland, the Housing Executive). They have a legal duty to offer help and advice, but will not offer you a place to live unless you have priority need (see above) and have a connection with the area, such as work or family. You must also show that you have not made yourself intentionally homeless.

## Help

If you are homeless or have problems with your landlord, help can be found from the following.

- The housing department of the local authority will give advice on homelessness and on Housing Benefit as well as deal with problems you may have in council-owned property.
- The Citizens Advice Bureau will give advice on all types of housing problems. There may also be a housing advice centre in your neighbourhood.
- Shelter is a housing charity which runs a 24-hour helpline on 0808 800 4444, or visit **www.shelter.org.uk**.
- Help with the cost of moving and setting up home may be available from the Social Fund. This is run by the Department for Work and Pensions (DWP). It provides grants and loans such as the Community Care Grant for people setting up home after being homeless or after they have been in prison or other institutions. Other loans are available for people who have had an emergency such as flooding. Information about these is available at the Citizens Advice Bureau or Jobcentre Plus.

---

HELPING YOU LEARN

**5.7** Where should you go for help if you are homeless in Northern Ireland?

**5.8** Is the following statement TRUE or FALSE?
The Citizens Advice Bureau will give advice on all types of housing problems.

---

**DID YOU KNOW?**

Did you know that the Citizens Advice Bureau is a charity? It has 20,000 people working as volunteers. They help over 5.5 million people a year and have 3,200 offices.

*Source*: www.citizensadvice.org.uk

---

**checklist** – Housing

Now you have read Section 1, can you remember the following?

■ The process for buying and renting accommodation.

■ Where to get advice about accommodation and moving.

■ The role of an estate agent.

■ Housing priorities for local authorities.

■ Where to get help if you are homeless.

# SECTION 2  Services in and for the home

In this section you will read about:

■ the services provided by local government;

■ council tax;

■ gas, electricity and water services and how to pay for them.

**Figure 5.2**   Electricity in the UK is supplied at 240 volts.

## Water

Water is supplied to all homes in the UK. The charge for this is called the water rates. When you move into a new home (bought or rented), you should receive a letter telling you the name of the company responsible for supplying your water. The water rates may be paid in one payment (a lump sum) or in instalments, usually monthly. If you receive Housing Benefit, you should check to see if this covers the water rates. The cost of the water usually depends on the size of your property, but some homes have a water meter, which tells you exactly how much water you have used. In Northern Ireland water is currently (2006) included in the domestic rates (see Council tax [page 112]), although this may change in future.

## Electricity and gas

All properties in the UK have electricity supplied at 240 volts. Most homes also have gas. When you move into a new home or leave an old one, you should make a note of the electricity and gas meter readings. If you have an urgent problem with your gas, electricity or water supply, you can ring a 24-hour helpline. This can be found on your bill, in the Yellow Pages or in the phone book.

---

### HELPING YOU LEARN

**5.9** Name TWO places where you can find the telephone number of a 24-hour helpline for your gas, electricity and water supply.

# Gas and electricity suppliers

It is possible to choose between different gas and electricity suppliers. These have different prices and different terms and conditions. Get advice before you sign a contract with a new supplier. To find out which company supplies your gas, telephone Transco on 0870 608 1524.

To find out which company supplies your electricity, telephone Energywatch on 0845 906 0708 or visit: **www.energywatch.org.uk**. Energywatch can also give you advice on changing your supplier of electricity or gas.

HELPING YOU LEARN

**5.10** Who can you phone to find out which company supplies your gas?

# Telephone

Most homes already have a telephone line (called a landline). If you need a new line, telephone BT on 150 442, or contact a cable company. Many companies offer landline, mobile telephone and broadband internet services. You can get advice about prices or about changing your company from Ofcom at: **www.ofcom.org.uk**. You can call from public payphones using cash, pre-paid phonecards or credit or debit cards. Calls made from hotels and hostels are usually more expensive. Dial 999 or 112 for emergency calls for police, fire or ambulance services. These calls are free. Do not use these numbers if it is not a real emergency; you can always find the local numbers for these services in the phone book.

# Bills

Information on how to pay for water, gas, electricity and the telephone is found on the back of each bill. If you have a bank account you can pay your bills by standing order or direct debit. Most companies operate a budget scheme, which allows you to pay a fixed sum every month. If you do not pay a bill, the service can be cut off. To get a service reconnected, you have to pay another charge.

HELPING YOU LEARN

**5.11** Which telephone numbers would you dial in an emergency to contact the police, fire or ambulance service?

## Refuse

Refuse is also called waste, or rubbish. The local authority collects the waste regularly, usually on the same day of each week. Waste must be put outside in a particular place to get collected. In some parts of the country the waste is put into plastic bags, in others it is put into bins with wheels. In many places you must recycle your rubbish, separating paper, glass, metal or plastic from the other rubbish. Large objects which you want to throw away, such as a bed, a wardrobe or a fridge, need to be collected separately. Contact the local authority to arrange this. If you have a business, such as a factory or a shop, you must make special arrangements with the local authority for your waste to be collected. It is a criminal offence to dump rubbish anywhere.

HELPING YOU LEARN

**5.12** Who do you contact if you want to throw away a large object such as a fridge?

## Council tax

Local government services, such as education, police, roads, refuse collection and libraries, are paid for partly by grants from the government and partly by council tax (see Chapter 4, Local government [page 84]). In Northern Ireland there is a system of domestic rates instead of the council tax. The amount of council tax you pay depends on the size and value of your house or flat (dwelling). You must register to pay council tax when you move into a new property, either as the owner or the tenant. You can pay the tax in one payment, in two instalments, or in ten instalments (from April to January).

If only one person lives in the flat or house, you get a 25% reduction on your council tax. (This does not apply in Northern Ireland.) You may also get a reduction if someone in the property has a disability. People on a low income or who receive benefits such as Income Support or Jobseeker's Allowance can get Council Tax Benefit. You can get advice on this from the local authority or the Citizens Advice Bureau.

HELPING YOU LEARN

**5.13** Which of the following statements is correct?
   **A.**   In England, if only one person lives in a flat or house, you get a 15% reduction on your council tax.
   **B.**   In England, if only one person lives in a flat or house, you get a 25% reduction on your council tax.
**5.14** In Figure 5.3, can you write TWO more services that local government provides?

**Figure 5.3**

Local government services

Roads

Libraries

Education

.................................................................

.................................................................

# Buildings and household insurance

If you buy a home with a mortgage, you must insure the building against fire, theft and accidental damage. The landlord should arrange insurance for rented buildings. It is also wise to insure your possessions against theft or damage. There are many companies that provide insurance.

# Neighbours

If you live in rented accommodation, you will have a tenancy agreement. This explains all the conditions of your tenancy. It will probably include information on what to do if you have problems with your housing. Occasionally, there may be problems with your neighbours. If you do have problems with your neighbours, they can usually be solved by speaking to them first. If you cannot solve the problem, speak to your landlord, local authority or housing association. Keep a record of the problems in case you have to show exactly what the problems are and when they started. Neighbours who cause a very serious nuisance may be taken to court and can be evicted from their home.

There are several mediation organisations which help neighbours to solve their disputes without having to go to court. Mediators talk to both sides and try to find a solution acceptable to both. You can get details of mediation organisations from the local authority, Citizens Advice, and Mediation UK on 0117 904 6661 or visit: **www.mediationuk.co.uk**.

**IMPORTANT** INFORMATION

The information in the handbook about Mediation UK is now out of date. It has been left in this guide because any of the information in the official handbook published by the Home Office can be included in the test.

**checklist** – Services in and for the home

Now you have read Section 2, can you remember the following?

■ How to recycle and dispose of your household waste.

■ Information about council tax and the local services it pays for.

■ When you should phone 999 or 112.

■ What to do if you have problems with your neighbours.

# SECTION 3  Money and credit

In this section you will read about:

■ financial services in the UK;

■ banks and building societies and the services they offer;

■ how the government helps people who do not have enough money to support themselves.

Banknotes in the UK come in denominations (values) of £5, £10, £20 and £50. Northern Ireland and Scotland have their own banknotes, which are valid everywhere in the UK, although sometimes people may not realise this and may not wish to accept them.

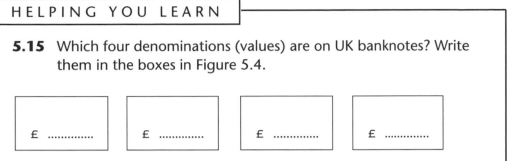

HELPING YOU LEARN

**5.15** Which four denominations (values) are on UK banknotes? Write them in the boxes in Figure 5.4.

£ ............. | £ ............. | £ ............. | £ .............

**Figure 5.4**

# The euro

In January 2002 twelve European Union (EU) states adopted the euro as their common currency. The UK government decided not to adopt the euro at that time, and has said it will only do so if the British people vote for the euro in a referendum. The euro does circulate to some extent in Northern Ireland, particularly in the towns near the border with Ireland.

## Foreign currency

You can get or change foreign currency at banks, building societies, large post offices and exchange shops or bureaux de change. You might have to order some currencies in advance. The exchange rates vary and you should check for the best deal.

## Banks and building societies

Most adults in the UK have a bank or building society account. Many large national banks or building societies have branches in towns and cities throughout the UK. It is worth checking the different types of account each one offers. Many employers pay salaries directly into a bank or building society. There are many banks and building societies to choose from. To open an account, you need to show documents to prove your identity, such as a passport, immigration document or driving licence. You also need to show something with your address on it like a tenancy agreement or household bill. It is also possible to open bank accounts in some supermarkets or on the internet.

---

HELPING YOU LEARN

**5.16** In which TWO of the following places can you get and change foreign currency?

   **A.**   Credit Union
   **B.**   Citizens Advice Bureau
   **C.**   Large post offices
   **D.**   Building societies

**5.17** Is the following statement TRUE or FALSE?

It is possible to open bank accounts in some supermarkets.

**Figure 5.5**

## Cash and debit cards

Cash cards allow you to use cash machines to withdraw money from your account. For this you need a Personal Identification Number (PIN), which you must keep secret. A debit card allows you to pay for things without using cash. You must have enough money in your account to cover what you buy. If you lose your cash card or debit card you must inform the bank immediately.

## Credit and store cards

Credit cards can be used to buy things in shops, on the telephone and over the internet. A store card is like a credit card but used only in a specific shop. Credit and store cards do not draw money from your bank account, but you will be sent a bill every month. If you do not pay the total amount on the bill, you are charged interest. Although credit and store cards are useful, the interest is usually very high and many people fall into debt this way. If you lose your credit or store cards you must inform the company immediately.

DID YOU KNOW?

**Did you know that there are 67.3 million credit cards currently in use in the UK?**

*Source*: uswitch.com

HELPING YOU LEARN

**5.18** Is the following statement TRUE or FALSE?
Credit and store cards usually have low interest rates.

# Credit and loans

People in the UK often borrow money from banks and other organisations to pay for things like household goods, cars and holidays. This is more common in the UK than in many other countries. You must be very sure of the terms and conditions when you decide to take out a loan. You can get advice on loans from the Citizens Advice Bureau if you are uncertain.

## Being refused credit
Banks and other organisations use different information about you to make a decision about a loan, such as your occupation, address, salary and previous credit record. If you apply for a loan you might be refused. If this happens, you have the right to ask the reason why.

## Credit unions
Credit unions are financial co-operatives owned and controlled by their members. The members pool their savings and then make loans from the pool. Interest rates in credit unions are usually lower than banks and building societies. There are credit unions in many cities and towns. To find the nearest credit union contact the Association of British Credit Unions (ABCUL) on: **www.abcul.coop**.

# Insurance

As well as insuring their property and possessions (see above), many people insure their credit cards and mobile phones. They also buy insurance when they travel abroad in case they lose their luggage or need medical treatment. Insurance is compulsory if you have a car or motorcycle. You can usually arrange insurance directly with an insurance company, or you can use a broker who will help you get the best deal.

## Social security

The UK has a system of social security, which pays welfare benefits to people who do not have enough money to live on. Benefits are usually available for the sick and disabled, older people, the unemployed and those on low incomes. People who do not have legal rights of residence (or 'settlement') in the UK cannot usually receive benefits. Arrangements for paying and receiving benefits are complex because they have to cover people in many different situations. Guides to benefits are available from Jobcentre Plus offices, local libraries, post offices and the Citizens Advice Bureau.

### HELPING YOU LEARN

**5.19** On the Social Security form in Figure 5.6 add TWO groups of people who are usually able to claim benefits.

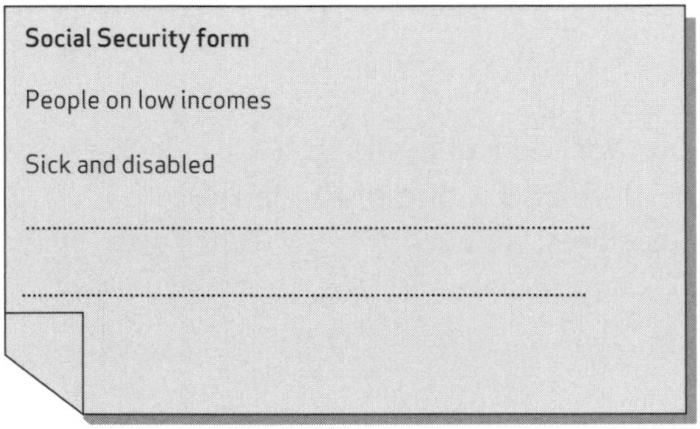

**Figure 5.6**

Social Security form

People on low incomes

Sick and disabled

..................................................................................

..................................................................................

### checklist – Money and credit

Now you have read Section 3, can you remember the following?

- **Which documents you need to open a bank or building society account.**
- **What debit, credit and store cards are.**
- **What a credit union is.**
- **What insurance is.**
- **How to get help if you have problems with debt.**

# SECTION 4 Health

In this section you will read about:

■ how healthcare is organised under the National Health Service (NHS);

■ how to get information and advice when you are unwell;

■ doctors, dentists and opticians;

■ care for pregnant women.

**IMPORTANT** INFORMATION

If you need to find a doctor there is important information in this section that will help you.

## Healthcare

Healthcare in the UK is organised under the National Health Service (NHS). The NHS began in 1948, and is one of the largest organisations in Europe. It provides all residents with free healthcare and treatment.

### Finding a doctor
Family doctors are called General Practitioners (GPs) and they work in surgeries. GPs often work together in a group practice. This is sometimes called a Primary Healthcare Centre.

Your GP is responsible for organising the health treatment you receive. Treatment can be for physical and mental illnesses. If you need to see a specialist, you must go to your GP first. Your GP will then refer you to a specialist in a hospital. Your GP can also refer you for specialist treatment if you have special needs.

You can get a list of local GPs from libraries, post offices, the tourist information office, the Citizens Advice Bureau, the local health authority and from the following websites:

■ **www.nhs.uk/** for health practitioners in England;
■ **www.wales.nhs.uk/directory.cfm** for health practitioners in Wales;
■ **www.n-i.nhs.uk** for health practitioners in Northern Ireland;
■ **www.show.scot.nhs.uk/** in Scotland.

You can also ask neighbours and friends for the name of their local doctor.

You can attend a hospital without a GP's letter only in the case of an emergency. If you have an emergency you should go to the Accident and Emergency (A & E) department of the nearest hospital.

HELPING YOU LEARN

**5.20** What do the letters GP stand for?

DID YOU KNOW?

**Did you know that the National Health Service (NHS) was started by a Labour Government after the Second World War?**
**It was introduced by Aneurin Bevan, the Minister for Health.**

# Registering with a GP

You should look for a GP as soon as you move to a new area. You should not wait until you are ill. The health centre, or surgery, will tell you what you need to do to register. Usually you must have a medical card. If you do not have one, the GP's receptionist should give you a form to send to the local health authority. They will then send you a medical card.

Before you register you should check that the surgery can offer what you need. For example, you might need a woman GP, or maternity services. Sometimes GPs have many patients and are unable to accept new ones. If you cannot find a GP, you can ask your local health authority to help you find one.

## Using your doctor

All patients registering with a GP are entitled to a free health check. Appointments to see the GP can be made by phone or in person. Sometimes you might have to wait several days before you can see a doctor. If you need immediate medical attention ask for an urgent appointment. You should go to the GP's surgery a few minutes before the appointment. If you cannot attend or do not need the appointment any more, you must let the surgery know. The GP needs patients to answer all questions as fully as possible in order to find out what is wrong. Everything you tell the GP is completely confidential and cannot be passed on to anyone else without your permission. If you do not understand something, ask for clarification. If you have difficulties with English, bring someone who can help you, or ask the receptionist for an interpreter. This must be done when you make the appointment. If you have asked for an interpreter, it is important that you keep your appointment because this service is expensive.

In exceptional circumstances, GPs can visit patients at home but they always give priority to people who are unable to travel. If you call the GP outside normal working hours, you will have to answer several questions about your situation. This is to assess how serious your case is. You will then be told if a doctor can come to your home. You might be advised to go to the nearest A & E department.

## Charges

Treatment from the GP is free but you have to pay a charge for your medicines and for certain services, such as vaccinations for travel abroad. If the GP decides you need to take medicine, you will be given a prescription. You must take this to a pharmacy (chemist).

## Prescriptions

Prescriptions are free for anyone who is:

- under 16 years of age (under 25 in Wales);
- under 19 and in full-time education;
- aged 60 or over;
- pregnant or with a baby under 12 months old;
- suffering from a specified medical condition;
- receiving Income Support, Jobseeker's Allowance, Working Families or Disabilities Tax Credit.

**Figure 5.7**

HELPING YOU LEARN

**5.21** On the form in Figure 5.8 on page 124, list THREE groups of people who do not need to pay for their prescriptions. To help you with this activity read the section on prescriptions again.

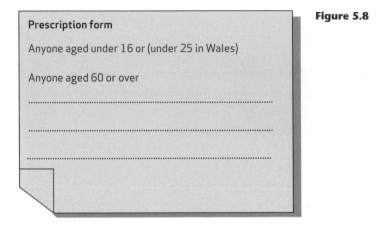

**Figure 5.8**

Prescription form

Anyone aged under 16 or (under 25 in Wales)

Anyone aged 60 or over

.......................................................................

.......................................................................

.......................................................................

# Feeling unwell

If you or your child feels unwell you have the following options:

## For information or advice
■ Ask your local pharmacist (chemist). The pharmacy can give advice on medicines and some illnesses and conditions that are not serious.
■ Speak to a nurse by phoning NHS Direct on 0845 46 47.
■ Use the NHS Direct website, NHS Direct Online: **www.nhsdirect.nhs.uk**.

## To see a doctor or nurse
■ Make an appointment to see your GP or a nurse working in the surgery.
■ Visit an NHS walk-in centre.

## For urgent medical treatment
■ Contact your GP.
■ Go to your nearest hospital with an Accident and Emergency department.
■ Call 999 for an ambulance. Calls are free. ONLY use this service for a real emergency.

NHS Direct is a 24-hour telephone service which provides information on particular health conditions. Telephone 0845 46 47. You may ask for an interpreter for advice in your own language. In Scotland, NHS24 at: **www.nhs24.com**, telephone 08454 24 24 24.

> NHS Direct Online is a website providing information about health services and several medical conditions and treatments: **www.nhsdirect.nhs.uk**.
>
> NHS walk-in centres provide treatment for minor injuries and illnesses seven days a week. You do not need an appointment. For details of your nearest centre call NHS Direct or visit the NHS website at: **www.nhs.uk** (for Northern Ireland **www.n-i.nhs.uk**) and click on 'local NHS services'.

## HELPING YOU LEARN

**5.22** In Figure 5.9 add other people or services you could contact in each of the three situations. An example has been included for each situation. Use the information in the study material to help you.

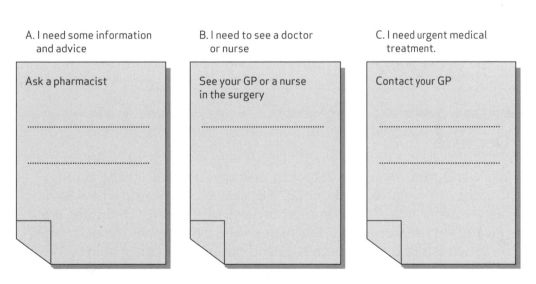

A. I need some information and advice

Ask a pharmacist

....................................................

....................................................

B. I need to see a doctor or nurse

See your GP or a nurse in the surgery

....................................................

C. I need urgent medical treatment.

Contact your GP

....................................................

....................................................

**Figure 5.9**

# Going into hospital

If you need minor tests at a hospital, you will probably attend the Outpatients department. If your treatment takes several hours, you will go into hospital as a day patient. If you need to stay overnight, you will go into hospital as an in-patient.

You should take personal belongings with you, such as a towel, night clothes, things for washing and a dressing gown. You will receive all your meals while you are an in-patient. If you need advice about going into hospital, contact Customer Services or the Patient Advice and Liaison Service (PALS) at the hospital where you will receive treatment.

HELPING YOU LEARN

**5.23** Look at the study material above and choose FOUR of these items to put in your overnight bag to take into hospital.

| Radio | Yes/No | Towel | Yes/No |
|---|---|---|---|
| Washing items | Yes/No | Jewellery | Yes/No |
| Dressing gown | Yes/No | Night clothes | Yes/No |

# Dentists

You can get the name of a dentist by asking at the local library, at the Citizens Advice Bureau and through NHS Direct. Most people have to pay for dental treatment. Some dentists work for the NHS and some are private. NHS dentists charge less than private dentists, but some dentists have two sets of charges, both NHS and private. A dentist should explain your treatment and the charges before the treatment begins.

Free dental treatment is available to:

■ people under 18 (in Wales people under 25 and over 60);
■ pregnant women and women with babies under 12 months old;
■ people on income support, Jobseeker's Allowance or Pension Credit Guarantee.

## Opticians

Most people have to pay for sight tests and glasses, except children, people over 60, people with certain eye conditions and people receiving certain benefits. In Scotland, eye tests are free.

## Pregnancy and care of young children

If you are pregnant you will receive regular antenatal care. This is available from your local hospital, local health centre or from special antenatal clinics. You will receive support from a GP and from a midwife. Midwives work in hospitals or health centres. Some GPs do not provide maternity services so you may wish to look for another GP during your pregnancy. In the UK women usually have their babies in hospital, especially if it is their first baby. It is common for the father to attend the birth, but only if the mother wants him to be there.

A short time after you have your child, you will begin regular contact with a health visitor. She or he is a qualified nurse and can advise you about caring for your baby. The first visits will be in your home, but after that you might meet the health visitor at a clinic. You can ask advice from your health visitor until your child is five years old. In most towns and cities there are mother and toddler groups or playgroups for small children. These often take place at local churches and community centres. You might be able to send your child to a nursery school.

## HELPING YOU LEARN

**5.24**  Is the following statement TRUE or FALSE?
People over 60 years of age don't have to pay for eye tests.

**5.25**  Name TWO places where antenatal care can be obtained?

**5.26**  Which of the following statements is correct?
**A.**  People under 25 in Wales receive free dental treatment.
**B.**  Dental treatment is free for people over 55 in Wales.

# Information on pregnancy

You can get information on maternity and antenatal services in your area from your local health authority, a health visitor or your GP. The number of your health authority will be in the phone book.

The Family Planning Association (FPA) gives advice on contraception and sexual health. The FPA's helpline is 0845 310 1334, or: **www.fpa.org.uk**.

The National Childbirth Trust gives information and support in pregnancy, childbirth and early parenthood: **www.nctpregnancyandbabycare.com**.

# Registering a birth

You must register your baby with the Registrar of Births, Marriages and Deaths (Register Office) within six weeks of the birth. The address of your local Register Office is in the phone book. If the parents are married, either the mother or father can register the birth. If they are not married, only the mother can register the birth. If the parents are not married but want both names on the child's birth certificate, both mother and father must be present when they register their baby.

---

**checklist** – Health

Now you have read Section 4, can you remember the following?

■ How to find and register with a GP.

■ What to do if you feel unwell.

■ How to find other services such as dentists and opticians.

■ When it is possible to attend hospital without a doctor's letter.

■ Who can get free prescriptions.

■ What NHS Direct can do.

■ Who can give health advice and treatment when you are pregnant and after you have a baby.

■ How to register a birth.

# SECTION 5 Education

In this section you will read about:

- the different types of schools, including state, independent and faith schools;

- what is included in the school curriculum and assessment methods;

- parents' responsibilities;

- further education.

## Going to school

Education in the UK is free and compulsory for all children between the ages of 5 and 16 (4 and 16 in Northern Ireland). The education system varies in England, Scotland, Wales and Northern Ireland.

The child's parent or guardian is responsible for making sure their child goes to school, arrives on time and attends for the whole school year. If they do not do this, the parent or guardian may be prosecuted.

Some areas of the country offer free nursery education for children over the age of 3. In most parts of the UK, compulsory education is divided into two stages, primary and secondary. In some places there is a middle-school system. In England and Wales the primary stage lasts from 5 to 11, in Scotland from 5 to 12 and in Northern Ireland from 4 to 11. The secondary stage lasts until the age of 16. At that age young people can choose to leave school or to continue with their education until they are 17 or 18.

Details of local schools are available from your local education authority office or website. The addresses and phone numbers of local education authorities are in the phone book.

HELPING YOU LEARN

**5.27** Between which ages is education compulsory in Northern Ireland?

# Primary schools

These are usually schools where both boys and girls learn together and are usually close to a child's home. Children tend to be with the same group and teacher all day. Schools encourage parents to help their children with learning, particularly with reading and writing.

# Secondary schools

At age 11 (12 in Scotland) children go to secondary school. This might normally be the school nearest their home, but parents in England and Wales are allowed to express a preference for a different school. In some areas, getting a secondary school place in a preferred school can be difficult, and parents often apply to several schools in order to make sure their child gets offered a place. In Northern Ireland many schools select children through a test taken at the age of 11.

If the preferred school has enough places, the child will be offered a place. If there are not enough places, children will be offered places according to the school's admissions arrangements. Admission arrangements vary from area to area.

Secondary schools are larger than primary schools. Most are mixed sex, although there are single-sex schools in some areas. Your local education authority will give you information on schools in your area. It will also tell you which schools have spaces and give you information about why some children will be given places when only a few are available and why other children might not. It will also tell you how to apply for a secondary school place.

## STUDY TIP

To help you remember the differences in the education system, why not draw timelines for England, Wales, Scotland and Northern Ireland showing the ages children start and finish different stages of their education?

You might also find it helpful to have another look in Chapter 2 at Figure 2.6 (page 35), which shows a summary of the education process.

## Costs

Education at state schools in the UK is free, but parents have to pay for school uniforms and sports wear. There are sometimes extra charges for music lessons and for school outings. Parents on low incomes can get help with costs, and with the cost of school meals. You can get advice on this from the local education authority or the Citizens Advice Bureau.

## Church and other faith schools

Some primary and secondary schools in the UK are linked to the Church of England or the Roman Catholic Church. These are called 'faith schools'. In some areas there are Muslim, Jewish and Sikh schools. In Northern Ireland, some schools are called Integrated Schools. These schools aim to bring children of different religions together. Information on faith schools is available from your local education authority.

## Independent schools

Independent schools are private schools. They are not run or paid for by the state. Independent secondary schools are also sometimes called public schools. There are about 2,500 independent schools in the UK. About 8% of children go to these schools. At independent schools parents must pay the full cost of their child's education. Some independent schools offer scholarships, which pay some or all of the costs of the child's education.

**5.28** In state schools, which TWO of the following are paid for by parents?

**A.** Books
**B.** School uniform
**C.** Examination fees
**D.** Sports wear

# The school curriculum

All state, primary and secondary schools in England, Wales and Northern Ireland follow the National Curriculum. This covers English, maths, science, design and technology, information and communication technology (ICT), history, geography, modern foreign languages, art and design, music, physical education (PE) and citizenship. In Wales, children learn Welsh.

In some primary schools in Wales, all the lessons are taught in Welsh. In Scotland, pupils follow a broad curriculum informed by national guidance. Schools must, by law, provide religious education (RE) to all pupils. Parents are allowed to withdraw their children from these lessons. RE lessons have a Christian basis but children also learn about the other major religions.

**5.29** Is the following statement TRUE or FALSE?
History is part of the National Curriculum.

## Assessment

In England, the curriculum is divided into four stages, called Key Stages. After each stage children are tested. They take Key Stage tests (also called SATs) at ages 7, 11 and 14. At 16 they usually take the General Certificates of Secondary Education (GCSEs) in several subjects, although some schools also offer other qualifications. At 18, young people who have stayed at school do AGCEs (Advanced GCE levels) often just called A Levels.

In Wales, schools follow the Welsh National Curriculum but have abolished national tests for children at ages 7 and 11. There are also plans in Wales to stop testing children at 14. Teachers in Wales still have to assess and report on their pupils' progress and achievements at 7 and 11.

In Scotland, the curriculum is divided into two phases. The first phase is from 5 to 14. There are six levels in this phase, levels A to F. There are no tests for whole groups during this time. Teachers test individual children when they are ready. From 14 to 16, young people do Standard Grade. After 16 they can study at Intermediate, Higher or Advanced Level. In Scotland there will soon be a single curriculum for all pupils from age 3 to age 18. This is called A Curriculum of Excellence. More information can be found at: **www.acurriculumforexcellencescotland.gov.uk**.

---

STUDY TIP

To help you remember how assessment differs in England, Scotland and Wales, you might find it easier to draw a diagram for England and Scotland like the one below.

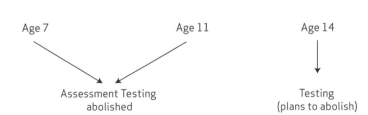

Welsh National Curriculum

Age 7                    Age 11                    Age 14

Assessment Testing              Testing
abolished                    (plans to abolish)

**Figure 5.10**

# Help with English

If your child's main language is not English, the school may arrange for extra language support from an EAL (English Additional Language) specialist teacher.

# Careers education

All children get careers advice from the age of 14. Advice is also available from Connexions, a national service for young people: telephone 080 800 13219 or: **www.connexions-direct.com** in England. In Wales, Careers Wales offers advice to children from the age of 11.  For further information visit: **www.careerswales.com** or telephone 0800 100 900.

In Scotland, Careers Scotland provides information, services and support to all ages and stages. For further information visit: **www.careers-scotland.org.uk** or telephone 0845 8 502 502.

# Parents and schools

Many parents are involved with their child's school. A number of places on a school's governing body are reserved for parents. The governing body decides how the school is run and administered, and produces reports on the progress of the school from year to year. In Scotland, parents can be members of school boards or parent councils.

Schools must be open 190 days a year. Term dates are decided by the governing body or by the local education authority. Children must attend the whole school year. Schools expect parents and guardians to inform them if their child is going to be absent from school. All schools ask parents to sign a home–school agreement. This is a list of things that both the school and the parent or guardian agree to do to ensure a good education for the child. All parents receive a report every year on their child's progress. They also have the chance to go to school to talk to their child's teachers.

**5.30** How many days a year must a school be open?

**5.31** Which of the following is a list of things that the school and the parent agree to do to ensure a good education for the child?

**A**. Home–school inventory

**B**. Home–school list

**C**. Home–school agreement

**D**. Home–school plan

# Further education and adult education

At 16, young people can leave school or stay on to do A Levels (Higher Grades in Scotland) in preparation for university. Some young people go to their local further education (FE) college to improve their exam grades or to get new qualifications for a career. Most courses are free up to the age of 19. Young people from families with low incomes can get financial help with their studies when they leave school at 16. This is called the Education Maintenance Allowance (EMA). Information about this is available at your local college or at: **www.dfes.gov.uk**.

Further education colleges also offer courses to adults over the age of 18. These include courses for people wishing to improve their skills in English. These courses are called ESOL (English for Speakers of Other Languages). There are also courses for English speakers who need to improve their literacy and numeracy and for people who need to learn new skills for employment. ESOL courses are also available in community centres and training centres. There is sometimes a waiting list for ESOL courses because demand is high. In England and Wales, ESOL, literacy and numeracy courses are also called *Skills for Life* courses. You can get information at your local college or local library or from Learndirect on 0800 100 900.

Many people join other adult education classes to learn a new skill or hobby and to meet new people. Classes are very varied and range from sports to learning a musical instrument or a new language. Details are usually available from your local library, college or adult education centre.

HELPING YOU LEARN

**5.32** What is ESOL the shortened term for?

**Figure 5.11**
An ESOL class.

## University

More young people go to university now than in the past. Many go after A Levels (or Higher Grades in Scotland) at age 18 but it is also possible to go to university later in life. At present, most students in England, Wales and Northern Ireland have to pay towards the cost of their tuition fees and to pay for their living expenses. In Scotland there are no tuition fees, but after students finish university they pay back some of the cost of their education in a payment called an endowment. At present, universities can charge up to £3,000 per year for their tuition fees, but students do not have to pay anything towards their fees before or during their studies. The government pays their tuition fees and then charges for them when a student starts working after university. Some families on low incomes receive help with their children's tuition fees. This is called a grant. The universities also give help, in the form of bursaries. Most students get a low-interest student loan from a bank. This pays for their living costs while they are at university. When a student finishes university and starts working, he or she must pay back the loan.

## HELPING YOU LEARN

**5.33** Up to how much a year can universities charge for their tuition fees?
- **A**. £2,000
- **B**. £1,000
- **C**. £1,500
- **D**. £3,000

## DID YOU KNOW?

**Did you know that the University of Manchester is the largest single-site university in the UK with 34,400 students?**
*Source*: www.manchester.ac.uk (Facts and Figures 2008)

## checklist – Education

Now you have read Section 5, can you remember the following?

■ **The different stages of a child's education.**

■ **That there are differences between the education systems in England, Scotland, Wales and Northern Ireland.**

■ **That there are different kinds of school, and that some of them charge fees.**

■ **What the National Curriculum is.**

■ **What the governing body of a school does.**

■ **Options for young people at the age of 16.**

■ **Courses available at FE colleges.**

■ **Where you can get English classes or other education for adults, including university.**

# SECTION 6 Leisure

In this section you will read about:

■ the UK system for classifying films;

■ TV licences;

■ the legal age at which young people can go into pubs, night clubs, betting shops and gambling clubs;

■ your responsibilities if you own a pet.

## Information

Information about theatre, cinema, music and exhibitions is found in local newspapers, local libraries and tourist information offices. Many museums and art galleries are free.

## Film, video and DVD

Films in the UK have a system to show if they are suitable for children. This is called the classification system. If a child is below the age of the classification, they should not watch the film at a cinema or on DVD. All films receive a classification, as follows.

**U** (Universal): suitable for anyone aged 4 years and over.

**PG** (parental guidance): suitable for everyone but some parts of the film might be unsuitable for children. Their parents should decide.

**12** or **12a**: children under 12 are not allowed to see or rent the film unless they are with an adult.

**15**: children under 15 are not allowed to see or rent the film.

**18**: no one under 18 is allowed to see or rent the film.

**R18**: no one under 18 is allowed to see the film, which is only available in specially licensed cinemas.

# Television and radio

Anyone in the UK with a television (TV), DVD or video recorder, computer or any device which is used for watching or recording TV programmes must be covered by a valid television licence. One licence covers all of the equipment at one address, but people who rent different rooms in a shared house must each buy a separate licence.

A colour TV licence costs £131.50 (2006) and lasts for 12 months. People aged 75 or over can apply for a free TV licence. Blind people can claim a 50% discount on their TV licence. You risk prosecution and a fine if you watch TV but are not covered by a TV licence. There are many ways to buy a TV licence, including from local Pay Point outlets or online at: **www.tvlicensing.co.uk**. It is also possible to pay for the licence in instalments. For more information, telephone 0870 576 3763 or write to TV Licensing, Bristol BS98 1TL.

HELPING YOU LEARN

**5.34** Is the following statement TRUE or FALSE?
People aged 75 or over can apply for a free TV licence.

## Sports, clubs and societies

Information about local clubs and societies can usually be found at local libraries or through your local authority. For information about sports you should ask in the local leisure centre. Libraries and leisure centres often organise activities for children during the school holidays.

## Places of interest

The UK has a large network of public footpaths in the countryside. Many parts of the countryside and places of interest are kept open by the National Trust. This is a charity that works to preserve important buildings and countryside in the UK. Information about National Trust buildings and areas open to the public is available on: **www.nationaltrust.org.uk**.

## Pubs and night clubs

Public houses, or pubs, are an important part of social life in the UK. To drink alcohol in a pub you must be 18 or over. People under 18 are not allowed to buy alcohol in a supermarket or in an off-licence either. The landlord of the pub may allow people of 14 to come into the pub but they are not allowed to drink. At 16, people can drink wine or beer with a meal in a hotel or restaurant.

Pubs are usually open during the day and until 11 p.m. If a pub wants to stay open later, it must apply for a special licence. Night clubs open and close later than pubs.

## Betting and gambling

People under 18 are not allowed into betting shops or gambling clubs. There is a National Lottery for which draws, with large prizes, are made every week. You can enter by buying a ticket or a scratch card. People under 16 are not allowed to buy a lottery ticket or scratch card.

**5.35**  At what age can young people do the following?

  **A.**  Drink alcohol in a pub  ........................

  **B.**  Buy alcohol in a supermarket  ........................

  **C.**  Drink wine or beer with a meal in a
  hotel or restaurant  ........................

  **D.**  Go into a betting shop  ........................

  **E.**  Buy a lottery ticket  ........................

## Pets

Many people in the UK have pets such as cats and dogs. It is against the law to treat a pet cruelly or to neglect it. All dogs in public places must wear a collar showing the name and address of the owner. The owner is responsible for keeping the dog under control and for cleaning up after the animal in a public place. Vaccinations and medical treatment for animals are available from veterinary surgeons (vets). If you cannot afford to pay a vet, you can go to a charity called the PDSA (People's Dispensary for Sick Animals). To find your nearest branch, visit: **www.pdsa.org.uk**.

**checklist** – Leisure

Now you have read Section 6, can you remember the following?

■ **How films are classified.**

■ **Why you need a television licence.**

■ **The rules about the selling and drinking of alcohol.**

# SECTION 7 Travel and transport

In this section you will read about:

- using public transport in the UK;

- the laws about driving in the UK;

- road tax and MOT tests;

- what to do if you are involved in an accident;

- different ways you can prove your identity.

---

## Trains, buses and coaches

For more information about trains, telephone the National Rail Enquiry Service: 08457 48 49 50, or visit: **www.nationalrail.co.uk**. For trains in Northern Ireland, phone Translink on 028 90 66 66 30 or visit: **www.translink.co.uk**. For information about local bus times, phone 0870 608 250. For information on coaches, telephone National Express on 08705 80 80 80, or visit: **www.nationalexpress.com**. For coaches in Scotland, telephone Scottish Citylink on 08705 50 50 50 or visit: **www.citylink.co.uk**. For Northern Ireland, visit: **www.translink.co.uk**.

Usually, tickets for trains and underground systems such as the London Underground must be bought before you get on the train. The fare varies according to the day and time you wish to travel. Travelling in the rush hour is always more expensive. Discount tickets are available for families, people aged 60 and over, disabled people, students and people under 26. Ask at your local train station for details. Failure to buy a ticket may result in a penalty.

---

HELPING YOU LEARN

**5.36** Without looking at the text, can you name THREE groups of people who can buy discount tickets for trains, buses and coaches?

## Taxis

To operate legally, all taxis and minicabs must be licensed and display a licence plate. Taxis and cabs with no licence are not insured for fare-paying passengers and are not always safe. Women should not use unlicensed minicabs.

DID YOU KNOW?

**Did you know that London taxi drivers must take a test called 'The Knowledge' before they can get a licence? To pass the test they need to know 320 routes in central London. This usually takes between two and four years to learn.**

*Source*: tfl.gov.uk

## Driving

You must be at least 17 to drive a car or motorcycle, 18 to drive a medium-sized lorry, and 21 to drive a large lorry or bus. To drive a lorry, minibus or bus with more than eight passenger seats, you must have a special licence.

HELPING YOU LEARN

**5.37** What age do you have to be to drive a large lorry or bus?

# The driving licence

You must have a driving licence to drive on public roads. To get a driving licence you must pass a test. There are many driving schools where you can learn with the help of a qualified instructor.

You get a full driving licence in three stages:

1. Apply for a provisional licence. You need this licence while you are learning to drive. With this you are allowed to drive a motorcycle up to 125cc or a car. You must put L plates on the vehicle, or D plates in Wales. Learner drivers cannot drive on a motorway. If you drive a car, you must be with someone who is over 21 and who has had a full licence for over three years. You can get an application form for a provisional licence from a post office.
2. Pass a written theory test.
3. Pass a practical driving test.

Drivers may use their licence until they are 70. After that the licence is valid for three years at a time.

In Northern Ireland, a newly qualified driver must display an R plate (for Registered driver) for one year after passing the test.

## HELPING YOU LEARN

**5.38**  Which of the following statements is correct?
>  **A.**  While you are learning to drive you must be with someone over 21 who has had a full licence for over three years.
>  **B.**  While you are learning to drive you must be with someone over 20 who has had a full licence for over 4 years.

## DID YOU KNOW?

**Did you know that the first section of motorway in the UK was only 8¼ miles long? It was opened in 1958 and it was called the Preston By-pass. It is now part of the M6 motorway in Lancashire.**

# Overseas licences

If your driving licence is from a country in the European Union (EU), Iceland, Liechtenstein or Norway, you can drive in the UK for as long as your licence is valid.

If you have a licence from a country outside the EU, you may use it in the UK for up to 12 months. During this time you must get a UK provisional driving licence and pass both the UK theory and practical driving tests, or you will not be able to drive after 12 months.

# Insurance

It is a criminal offence to have a car without proper motor insurance. Drivers without insurance can receive very high fines. It is also illegal to allow someone to use your car if they are not insured to drive it.

# Road tax and MOT

You must also pay a tax to drive your car on the roads. This is called road tax. Your vehicle must have a road tax disc, which shows you have paid. You can buy this at the post office. If you do not pay the road tax, your vehicle may be clamped or towed away.

If your vehicle is over three years old, you must take it every year for a Ministry of Transport (MOT) test. You can do this at an approved garage. The garage will give you an MOT certificate when your car passes the test. It is an offence not to have an MOT certificate. If you do not have an MOT certificate, your insurance will not be valid.

HELPING YOU LEARN

**5.39** In Figure 5.12 on page 146 list the THREE other documents you require to drive a car on a public road in the UK. The first one has been completed for you.

**Figure 5.12**

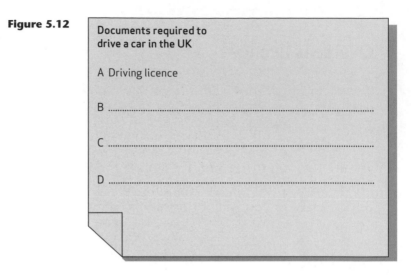

Documents required to
drive a car in the UK

A Driving licence

B ............................................................................

C ............................................................................

D ............................................................................

## Safety

Everyone in a vehicle should wear a seat belt. Children under 12 years of
age may need a special booster seat. Motorcyclists and their passengers
must wear a crash helmet (this law does not apply to Sikh men if they
are wearing a turban). It is illegal to drive while holding a mobile phone.

## Speed limits

For cars and motorcycles the speed limits are:

- 30 miles per hour (mph) in built-up areas, unless a sign shows a
  different limit;
- 60 mph on single carriageways;
- 70 mph on motorways and dual carriageways.

Speed limits are lower for buses, lorries and cars pulling caravans.

It is illegal to drive when you are over the alcohol limit or drunk. The
police can stop you and give you a test to see how much alcohol you
have in your body. This is called a breathalyser test. If a driver has more
than the permitted amount of alcohol (called being 'over the limit') or
refuses to take the test, he or she will be arrested. People who drink and
drive can expect to be disqualified from driving for a long period.

**5.40** What is the speed limit on motorways and dual carriageways?
- **A.** 60 miles per hour
- **B.** 65 miles per hour
- **C.** 70 miles per hour
- **D.** 80 miles per hour

# Accidents

If you are involved in a road accident:

- don't drive away without stopping – this is a criminal offence;
- call the police and ambulance on 999 or 112 if someone is injured;
- get the names, addresses, vehicle registration numbers and insurance details of the other drivers;
- give your details to the other drivers or passengers and to the police;
- make a note of everything that happened and contact your insurance company as soon as possible.

Note that, if you admit the accident was your fault, the insurance company may refuse to pay. It is better to wait until the insurance company decides for itself whose fault the accident was.

**5.41** What should you do if you are involved in an accident and someone is injured?

# Identity documents

At present, UK citizens do not have carry identity (ID) cards. The government is, however, making plans to introduce them in the next few years.

### Proving your identity

You may have to prove your identity at different times, such as when you open a bank account, rent accommodation, enrol for a college course, hire a car, apply for benefits such as housing benefit or apply for a marriage certificate. Different organisations may ask for different documents as proof of identity. These can include:

■ official documents from the Home Office showing your immigration status;
■ a certificate of identity;
■ a passport or travel document;
■ a National Insurance (NI) number card;
■ a provisional or full driving licence;
■ a recent gas, electricity or phone bill showing your name and address;
■ a rent or benefits book.

HELPING YOU LEARN

**5.42** Is the following statement TRUE or FALSE?
UK citizens have to carry ID cards.

**checklist** – Travel and transport

Now you have read Section 7, can you remember the following?

■ **How to get a driving licence.**

■ **What you need to do to be allowed to drive a vehicle in the UK.**

■ **What you should do if you have a road accident.**

■ **When you might have to prove your identity, and how you can do it.**

# SECTION 8 Revision questions and end of chapter checklist

Now you have finished reading the official study material, try to answer the following questions to see how much of Chapter 5 you can remember. If you are unsure of the answers, check your notes and refer back to the text before looking at the answers at the end of the book.

## Revision Questions for Chapter 5

1. Approximately what proportion of people in the UK own their own home?

Answer_____

2. How is the amount of council tax you pay calculated?

Answer_____

3. Which organisation can you contact if you have problems with your neighbours?

Answer_____

4. At what age do children in Scotland start secondary school?

Answer_____

5. What is the speed limit for driving on single carriageways in the UK?

Answer_____

6. After the age of 70 how long is a driving licence valid for?

Answer_____

7. How old must young people be to go into betting shops or gambling clubs?

Answer_____

8. Are English and maths covered in the National Curriculum?

Answer_____

9. Do people aged 60 or over have to pay for their prescriptions?

Answer_____

10. If you have a cat or a dog that is not well and you cannot afford to take it to a veterinary surgeon, which charity can you go to for help?

Answer_____

11. At what age can young people drink wine or beer with a meal in a hotel or restaurant?

Answer_____

12. Who is responsible for the collection and disposal of waste?

Answer_____

13. What does EMA stand for?

Answer_____

14. Are eye tests free in Scotland?

Answer_____

---

**End of Chapter 5 checklist**

Now that you have come to the end of Chapter 5, tick the boxes when you have:

- ■ read the study material;                                              ☐
- ■ made short notes to help you with your revision;                      ☐
- ■ made a note and checked words that you do not understand;             ☐
- ■ completed the *Helping you learn* and revision questions and checked your answers;    ☐
- ■ gone back and read again the sections for the questions you got wrong.    ☐

Well done, you have nearly finished the study material – only one more chapter to go.

## Answers to *Helping you learn* questions for Chapter 5

5.1   With a mortgage
5.2   False – a solicitor provides this service
5.3   A
5.4   The local authority
      Housing associations
      Private property owners (landlords)
5.5   One month's rent
5.6   A
5.7   The Housing Executive
5.8   True
5.9   On your bill
      Yellow Pages
      Phone book
5.10  Transco
5.11  999 or 112
5.12  Local authority
5.13  B
5.14  Police
      Refuse collection
5.15  £5, £10, £20, £50
5.16  C and D
5.17  True
5.18  False
5.19  Older people
      Unemployed
5.20  General Practitioner
5.21  Anyone under 19 and in full-time education
      Anyone pregnant or with a baby under 12 months old
      Anyone suffering from a specified medical condition
      Anyone receiving Income Support, Jobseeker's Allowance, Working
      Families or Disabilities Tax Credit
5.22  A    Phone NHS Direct
           Use the NHS Direct website
      B    Visit an NHS walk-in centre
      C    Go to the nearest A & E Department
           Call 999 for an ambulance

5.23   Washing items
       Towel
       Dressing gown
       Night clothes
5.24   True
5.25   Local hospital
       Local health centre
       Special antenatal clinics
5.26   A
5.27   4 to 16
5.28   B and D
5.29   True
5.30   190
5.31   C
5.32   English for Speakers of Other Languages
5.33   D
5.34   True
5.35   A      18
       B      18
       C      16
       D      18
       E      16
5.36   Families
       People aged over 60
       Disabled people
       Students
       People under 26
5.37   21
5.38   A
5.39   Insurance
       MOT certificate (if the vehicle is over three years old)
       Road tax disc
5.40   C
5.41   Call the police and ambulance by phoning 999 or 112
5.42   False – UK citizens are not required to carry ID cards

# Employment

In this chapter you will find information about the employment process, how to complete application forms and what to expect in a job interview.

There is information about your rights in the workplace and details about the support available if you lose your job.

In addition, you will read about the legal rights and entitlements of new mothers and fathers, and information about the laws relating to child employment.

To make it easier for you to remember the information this chapter is divided into six sections.

**Section 1** Looking for work.

**Section 2** Equal rights and discrimination.

**Section 3** At work.

**Section 4** Working for yourself.

**Section 5** Childcare and children at work.

**Section 6** Revision questions and end of chapter checklist.

## IMPORTANT INFORMATION

This chapter contains useful information about your rights and responsibilities at work. It also contains helpful advice if you are looking for work and applying for jobs.

# SECTION 1 Looking for work

In this section you will read about:

■ what to do if you are looking for work;

■ how to apply for jobs;

■ what to expect in a job interview;

■ overseas qualifications and their comparison with UK qualifications.

## Looking for work

If you are looking for work, or you are thinking of changing your job, there are a number of ways you can find out about work opportunities. The Home Office provides guidance on who is allowed to work in the UK. Not everyone in the UK is allowed to work and some people need work permits, so it is important to check your status before taking up work. Also, employers have to check that anyone they employ is legally entitled to work in the UK. For more information and guidance, see the Home Office website 'Working in the UK': **www.ukba.homeoffice.gov.uk/workingintheuk/**.

Jobs are usually advertised in local and national newspapers, at the local Jobcentre and in employment agencies. You can find the address and telephone number of your local Jobcentre under Jobcentre Plus in the phone book or see: **www.jobcentreplus.gov.uk**. Some jobs are advertised on supermarket notice boards and in shop windows. These jobs are usually part-time and the wages are often quite low. If there are particular companies you would like to work for, you can look for vacancies on their websites.

Jobcentre Plus is run by a government department – the Department for Work and Pensions. Trained staff give advice and help in finding and applying for jobs as well as claiming benefits. They can also arrange for interpreters. Their website **www.jobcentreplus.gov.uk** lists vacancies and training opportunities and gives general information on benefits. There is also a low-cost telephone service – Jobseeker Direct, 0845 60 60 234. This is open 9 a.m. to 6 p.m. on weekdays and 9 a.m. to 1 p.m. on Saturdays.

**Figure 6.1**

---

┌─────────────────────────────┐
│ H E L P I N G   Y O U   L E A R N │
└─────────────────────────────┘

**6.1** Which of the following statements is correct?
   **A.** Jobcentres provide guidance on who is allowed to work in the UK.
   **B.** The Home Office provides guidance on who is allowed to work in the UK.

**6.2** Look at the study material and name THREE places where jobs are advertised.
   When you have completed these questions you can check your answers at the end of the chapter.

## Qualifications

Applicants for some jobs need special training or qualifications. If you have qualifications from another country, you can find out how they compare with qualifications in the UK at the National Academic Recognition Information Centre (NARIC), **www.naric.org.uk**.

For further information, contact UK NARIC ECCTIS Ltd, Oriel House, Oriel Road, Cheltenham, Glos, GL50 1XP, telephone: 0870 990 4088, email: **info@naric.org.uk**.

## Applications

Interviews for lower paid and local jobs can often be arranged by telephone or in person. For many jobs you need to fill in an application form or send a copy of your curriculum vitae (CV) with a covering letter or letter of application.

A covering letter is usually a short letter attached to a completed application form, while a letter of application gives more detailed information on why you are applying for the job and why you think you are suitable. Your CV gives specific details on your education, qualifications, previous employment, skills and interests. It is important to type any letters and your CV on a computer or word processor as this improves your chance of being called for an interview.

Employers often ask for the names and addresses of one or two referees. These are people such as your current or previous employer or college tutor. Referees need to know you well and to agree to write a short report or reference on your suitability for the job. Personal friends or members of your family are not normally acceptable as referees.

HELPING YOU LEARN

**6.3** Look at the study material and in Figure 6.2 add THREE further details that you should include when you are applying for a job.

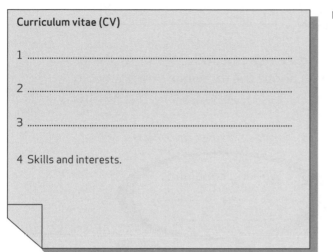

**Figure 6.2**

Curriculum vitae (CV)

1 ...........................................................................

2 ...........................................................................

3 ...........................................................................

4 Skills and interests.

# Interviews

In job descriptions and interviews, employers should give full details of what the job involves, including the pay, holidays and working conditions. If you need more information about any of these, you can ask questions in the interview. In fact, asking some questions in the interview shows you are interested and can improve your chance of getting the job.

When you are applying for a job and during the interview, it is important to be honest about your qualifications and experience. If an employer later finds out that you gave incorrect information, you might lose your job.

DID YOU KNOW?

Did you know that body language is very important in a job interview? For example, if you sit with your arms and legs crossed it gives the impression that you are not open to new ideas. Making eye contact with the interviewer is essential.

HELPING YOU LEARN

**6.4**   Look at the picture in Figure 6.3 and add TWO other things an employer should tell you about the job when you are being interviewed.

**Figure 6.3**

> Working conditions
>
> ....................................................
>
> ...............................................

## Criminal record

For some jobs, particularly if the work involves working with children or vulnerable people, the employer will ask for your permission to do a criminal record check. You can get more information on this from the Home Office Criminal Records Bureau (CRB) information line, telephone 0870 90 90 811. In Scotland, contact Disclosure Scotland: **www.disclosurescotland.co.uk**, Helpline: 0870 609 6006.

# Training

Taking up training helps people improve their qualifications for work. Some training may be offered at work or you can do courses from home or at your local college. This includes English language training. You can get more information from your local library and college or from websites such as **www.worktrain.gov.uk** and **www.learndirect.co.uk**. Learndirect offers a range of online training courses at centres across the country. There are charges for courses but you can do free starter or taster sessions. You can get more information from their free information and advice line: 0800 100 900.

# Volunteering and work experience

Some people do voluntary work and this can be a good way to support your local community and organisations which depend on volunteers. It also provides useful experience that can help with future job applications. Your local library will have more information about volunteering opportunities.

You can also get information and advice from websites such as: **www.do-it.org.uk**, **www.volunteering.org.uk** and **www.dosomething.org**.

---

**checklist** – Looking for work

Now you have read Section 1, can you remember the following?

- ■ **That the Home Office provides guidance on who is entitled to work in the UK.**
- ■ **That NARIC can advise on how qualifications from overseas compare with qualifications from the UK.**
- ■ **What CVs are.**
- ■ **Who can be a referee.**
- ■ **What happens if any of the information you have given is untrue.**

■ When you need a CRB check.

■ Where you can find out about training opportunities and job seeking.

■ The benefits of volunteering in terms of work experience and community involvement.

# SECTION 2 Equal rights and discrimination

In this section you will read about:

■ the laws relating to equal rights and discrimination;

■ the different forms sexual harassment can take and how to deal with the problem.

## Equal rights and discrimination

It is against the law for employers to discriminate against someone at work. This means that a person should not be refused work, training or promotion or treated less favourably because of their:

■ sex;
■ nationality, race, colour or ethnic group;
■ disability;
■ religion;
■ sexual orientation;
■ age.

In Northern Ireland, the law also bans discrimination on the grounds of religious belief or political opinion.

The law also says that men and women who do the same job, or work of equal value, should receive equal pay. Almost all the laws protecting people at work apply equally to people doing part-time or full-time jobs.

There are, however, a small number of jobs where discrimination laws do not apply. For example, discrimination is not against the law when the job involves working for someone in their own home.

You can get more information about the law and racial discrimination from the Commission for Racial Equality. The Equal Opportunities Commission can help with sex discrimination issues and the Disability Rights Commission deals with disability issues. Each of these organisations offers advice and information and can, in some cases, support individuals. From October 2007 their functions will be brought together in a new Commission for Equality and Human Rights. You can get more information about the laws protecting people at work from the Citizens Advice Bureau website: **www.adviceguide.org.uk**.

In Northern Ireland, the Equality Commission provides information and advice in respect of all forms of unlawful discrimination.

The Commission for Racial Equality, St Dunstan's House, 201–211 Borough High Street, London, SE1 1GZ, telephone: 020 7939 000, fax: 020 7939 0001, **www.cre.gov.uk**.

The Equal Opportunities Commission, Arndale House, Arndale Centre, Manchester M4 3EQ, telephone : 0845 601 5901, fax: 0161 838 8312, **www.eoc.org.uk**.

The Disability Rights Commission, DRC Helpline, FREEPOST MID02164, Stratford upon Avon CV37 9BR, telephone: 08457 622 633, fax: 08457 778 878, **www.drc.org.uk**.

The Equality Commission for Northern Ireland, Equality House, 7–9 Shaftsbury Square, Belfast BT2 7DP, telephone: 028 90 500600, **www.equalityni.org**.

## IMPORTANT INFORMATION

The following three organisations named above:

■ the Commission for Racial Equality;

■ the Equal Opportunities Commission; and

■ the Disability Rights Commission

have now joined together and formed the Equality and Human Rights Commission. Details are on their website: www.equalityhumanrights.com.

Remember, you will not be tested on this new organisation. You will only be tested on the information in the official study material even if it is now out of date.

## Sexual harassment

Sexual harassment can take different forms. This includes:

- indecent remarks;
- comments about the way you look that make you feel uncomfortable or humiliated;
- comments or questions about your sex life;
- inappropriate touching or sexual demands;
- bullying behaviour or being treated in a way that is rude, hostile, degrading or humiliating because of your sex.

Men and women can be victims of sexual harassment at work. If this happens to you, tell a friend, colleague or trade union representative and ask the person harassing you to stop. It is a good idea to keep a written record of what happened, the days and times when it happened and who else may have seen or heard the harassment. If the problem continues, report the person to your employer or trade union. Employers are responsible for the behaviour of their employees while they are at work. They should treat complaints of sexual harassment very seriously and take effective action to deal with the problem. If you are not satisfied with your employer's response, you can ask for advice and support from the Equal Opportunities Commission, your trade union or the Citizens Advice Bureau.

---

HELPING YOU LEARN

**6.5** Is the following statement TRUE or FALSE?
Men can be victims of sexual harassment at work.

| **checklist** – Equal rights and discrimination |
|---|

Now you have read Section 2, can you remember the following?

- **The law relating to discrimination in the workplace.**

- **The law relating to equal job and equal pay regardless of gender.**

- **The different commissions working to promote equal opportunities.**

- **The grounds for sexual harassment complaints.**

# SECTION 3 At work

In this section you will read about:

- **employers' and employees' legal responsibilities and contracts of employment;**

- **pay, holidays, tax, national insurance and pensions;**

- **employers' and employees' responsibilities for health and safety issues at work;**

- **losing your job, unfair dismissal, redundancy and unemployment.**

## At work

Both employers and employees have legal responsibilities at work. Employers have to pay employees for the work that they do, treat them fairly and take responsible care for their health and safety. Employees should do their work with reasonable skill, and care and follow all reasonable instructions. They should not damage their employer's business.

### A written contract or statement
Within two months of starting a new job, your employer should give you a written contract or statement with all the details and conditions

for your work. This should include your responsibilities, pay, working hours, holidays, sick pay and pension. It should also include the period of notice that both you and your employer should give for the employment to end. The contract or written statement is an important document and is very useful if there is ever a disagreement about your work, pay or conditions.

### Pay, hours and holidays

Your pay is agreed between you and your employer. There is a minimum wage in the UK that is a legal right for every employed person above compulsory school leaving age. The compulsory school leaving age is 16, but the time in the school year when 16 year olds can leave school in England and Wales is different from that in Scotland and Northern Ireland.

There are different minimum wage rates for different age groups. From October 2006 the rates are as follows:

- for workers aged 22 and above – £5.35 an hour;
- for 18–21 year olds – £4.45 an hour;
- for 16–17 year olds – £3.30 an hour.

Employers who pay their workers less than this are breaking the law. You can get more information from the Central Office of Information Directgov website, **www.direct.gov.uk**, which has a wide range of public service information. Alternatively, you can telephone the National Minimum Wage Helpline: 0845 600 0678.

Your contract or statement will show the number of hours you are expected to work. Your employer might ask if you can work more hours than this and it is your decision whether or not you do. Your employer cannot require you to work more hours than the hours agreed on your contract.

If you need to be absent from work, for example if you are ill or have a medical appointment, it is important to tell your employer as soon as you can in advance. Most employees who are 16 or over are entitled to at least four weeks paid holiday every year. This includes time for national holidays (see Chapter 3 [pages 58–60]). Your employer must give you a pay slip, or a similar written statement, each time you are paid. This must show exactly how much money has been taken off for tax and national insurance contributions.

**6.6** Look at Figure 6.4 and insert the correct minimum wage for the three age ranges.

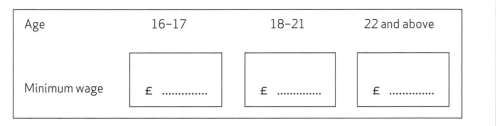

| Age | 16–17 | 18–21 | 22 and above |
| --- | --- | --- | --- |
| Minimum wage | £ .............. | £ .............. | £ .............. |

**Figure 6.4**

# Tax

For most people, tax is automatically taken from their earnings by the employer and paid directly to HM Revenue and Customs, the government department responsible for collecting taxes. If you are self-employed, you need to pay your own tax. Money raised from income tax pays for government services such as roads, education, police and the armed forces. Occasionally HM Revenue and Customs sends out tax returns forms, which ask for full financial details. If you receive one, it is important to complete it and return the form as soon as possible. You can get help and advice from the HM Revenue and Customs self-assessment helpline on 0845 300 45 55.

IMPORTANT INFORMATION

If you need to contact the HM Revenue and Customs self-assessment helpline the number has now changed to 0845 900 0444.

# National Insurance

Almost everybody in the UK who is in paid work, including self-employed people, must pay National Insurance (NI) contributions. Money raised from NI contributions is used to pay contributory benefits such as the State Retirement Pension and helps fund the National Health Service. Employees have their NI contributions deducted from their pay by their employer every week or month. People who are self-employed need to pay NI contributions themselves: Class 2 contributions, either by direct debit or every three months and Class 4 contributions on the profits from their trade or business. Class 4 contributions are paid alongside their income tax. Anyone who does not pay enough NI contributions will not be able to receive certain benefits, such as Jobseeker's Allowance or Maternity Pay, and may not receive a full State Retirement Pension.

**Getting a National Insurance number**
Just before their sixteenth birthday, all young people in the UK are sent a National Insurance number. This is a unique number for each person and it tracks their National Insurance contributions.

Refugees whose asylum applications have been successful have the same rights to work as any other UK citizen and to receive a National Insurance number. People who have applied for asylum and have not yet received a positive decision do not usually have permission to work and so do not get a National Insurance number.

You need a National Insurance number when you start work. If you do not have a National Insurance number, you can apply for one through Jobcentre Plus or your local Social Security office. It is a good idea to make an appointment by telephone and ask which documents you need to take with you. You usually need to show your birth certificate, passport and Home Office documents allowing you to stay in the country. If you need information about registering for a National Insurance number, you can telephone the National Insurance Registration Helpline on 0845 91 57006 or 0845 91 55670.

**6.7** At what age are all young people in the UK sent a National Insurance number?

**6.8** Which government department is responsible for collecting taxes?
A. Home Office
B. Treasury
C. HM Revenue and Customs
D. Local authority

# Pensions

Everyone in the UK who has paid enough National Insurance contributions will get a State Pension when they retire. The State Pension age for men is currently 65 years of age and for women it is 60, but the State Pension age for women will increase to 65 in stages between 2010 and 2020. You can find full details of the State Pension scheme on the State Pension website, **www.thepensionservice.gov.uk**, or you can phone the Pension Service Helpline: 0845 60 60 265.

In addition to a State Pension, many people also receive a pension through their work and some also pay into a personal pension plan too. It is very important to get good advice about pensions. The Pensions Advisory Service gives free and confidential advice on occupational and personal pensions. Their helpline telephone number is 0845 601 2923 and their website address is **www.opas.org.uk**. Independent financial advisers can also give advice but you usually have to pay a fee for this service. You can find local financial advisers in the Yellow Pages and Thomson local guides or on the internet at **www.unbiased.co.uk**.

**6.9** At what age do men in the UK receive the State Pension?

## Health and safety

Employers have a legal duty to make sure the workplace is safe. Employees also have a legal duty to follow safety regulations and to work safely and responsibly. If you are worried about health and safety at your workplace, talk to your supervisor, manager or trade union representative. You need to follow the right procedures and your employer must not dismiss you or treat you unfairly for raising a concern.

## Trade unions

Trade unions are organisations that aim to improve the pay and working conditions of their members. They also give their members advice and support on problems at work. You can choose whether to join a trade union or not, and your employer cannot dismiss you or treat you unfairly for being a union member.

You can find details of trade unions in the UK, the benefits they offer to members and useful information on rights at work on the Trades Unions Congress (TUC) website: **www.tuc.org.uk**.

HELPING YOU LEARN

**6.10** Without looking at the text, can you name TWO aims of trade union organisations?

**6.11** Is the following statement TRUE or FALSE?
British citizens are not allowed to work in other countries that are members of the European Economic Area (EEA).

# Problems at work

If you have problems of any kind at work, speak to your supervisor, manager, trade union representative or someone else with responsibility as soon as possible. If you need to take any action, it is a good idea to get advice first. If you are a member of a trade union, your representative will help. You can also contact your local Citizens Advice Bureau (CAB) or Law Centre. The national Advisory, Conciliation and Arbitration Service (ACAS) website, **www.acas.org.uk,** gives information on your rights at work. ACAS also offers a national helpline, telephone: 08457 47 47 47.

### Losing your job and unfair dismissal

An employee can be dismissed immediately for serious misconduct at work. Anyone who cannot do their job properly, or is unacceptably late or absent from work, should be given a warning by their employer. If their work, punctuality or attendance does not improve, the employer can give them notice to leave their job.

It is against the law for employers to dismiss someone from work unfairly. If this happens to you, or life at work is made so difficult that you feel you have to leave, you may be able to get compensation if you take your case to an Employment Tribunal. This is a court which specialises in employment matters. You normally only have three months to make a complaint.

If you are dismissed from your job, it is important to get advice on your case as soon as possible. You can ask for advice and information on your legal rights and the best action to take from your trade union representative, a solicitor, a Law Centre or the Citizens Advice Bureau.

### Redundancy

If you lose your job because the company you work for no longer needs someone to do your job, or cannot afford to employ you, you may be entitled to redundancy pay. The amount of money you receive depends on the length of time you have been employed. Again your trade union representative, a solicitor, a Law Centre or the Citizens Advice Bureau can advise you.

HELPING YOU LEARN

**6.12** In Figure 6.5 insert THREE places where you can get legal advice and information if you are dismissed from your job.

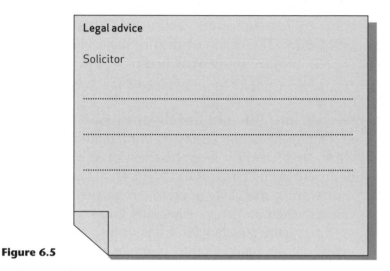

Legal advice

Solicitor

........................................................................

........................................................................

........................................................................

**Figure 6.5**

# Unemployment

Most people who become unemployed can claim Jobseeker's Allowance (JSA). This is currently available for men aged 18–65 and women aged 18–60 who are capable of working, available for work and trying to find work. Unemployed 16- and 17-year-olds may not be eligible for Jobseeker's Allowance but may be able to claim a Young Person's Bridging Allowance (YPBA) instead. The local Jobcentre Plus can help with claims. You can get further information from the Citizens Advice Bureau and the Jobcentre Plus website: **www.jobcentreplus.gov.uk**.

**New Deal**
New Deal is a government programme that aims to give unemployed people the help and support they need to get into work. Young people who have been unemployed for 6 months and adults who have been unemployed for 18 months are usually required to join New Deal if they wish to continue receiving benefit. There are different New Deal

schemes for different age groups. You can find out more about the New Deal on 0845 606 2626 or **www.newdeal.gov.uk**.

The government also runs work-based learning programmes which offer training to people while they are at work. People receive a wage or an allowance and can attend college for one day a week to get a new qualification.

You can find out more about the different government schemes, and the schemes in your area, from Jobcentre Plus, **www.jobcentreplus.gov.uk**, or your local Citizens Advice Bureau.

**IMPORTANT** INFORMATION

The website for New Deal, www.newdeal.gov.uk, is no longer in use.

**checklist** – At work

Now you have read Section 3, can you remember the following?

■ The importance of employment contracts.

■ The minimum wage and holiday entitlement.

■ What is deducted from your earnings and why.

■ The difference between being self-employed and employed.

■ Where to get help if you have problems at work.

■ The purpose of National Insurance and what happens if you don't pay enough contributions.

■ How you get a National Insurance number.

■ Who is entitled to a pension.

■ At what age men and women get a State Pension.

■ Employer and employee obligations for health and safety.

■ What trade unions are and who can join.

■ Possible reasons for dismissal.

■ Entitlement to redundancy pay.

# SECTION 4 Working for yourself

In this section you will read about:

■ your responsibilities for tax and national insurance;

■ where to get information and advice if you are self-employed.

## Tax

Self-employed people are responsible for paying their own tax and National Insurance. They have to keep detailed records of what they earn and spend on the business and send their business accounts to HM Revenue and Customs every year. Most self-employed people use an accountant to make sure they pay the correct tax and claim all the possible tax allowances.

As soon as you become self-employed you should register yourself for tax and National Insurance by ringing the HM Revenue and Customs telephone helpline for people who are self-employed, on 0845 915 4515.

### Help and advice
Banks can give information and advice on setting up your own business and offer start-up loans, which need to be repaid with interest. Government grants and other financial support may be available. You can get details of these and advice on becoming self-employed from Business Link, a government-funded project for people starting or running a business: **www.businesslink.gov.uk**, telephone: 0845 600 9006.

## Working in Europe

British citizens can work in any country that is a member of the European Economic Area (EEA). In general, they have the same employment rights as a citizen of that country or state.

---

**HELPING YOU LEARN**

**6.13** Which government-funded project provides advice on becoming self-employed?

   **A.** New Deal

   **B.** Business Link

   **C.** Job Centre Plus

   **D.** HM Revenue and Customs

---

**checklist** – Working for yourself

Now you have read Section 4, can you remember the following?

■ **Your responsibility for keeping detailed records and paying tax and national insurance.**

■ **The role of Business Link.**

# SECTION 5  Childcare and children at work

In this section you will read about:

■ **the laws concerning the employment of children;**

■ **the responsibilities of employers and parents;**

■ **your right to time off work as a new parent.**

## New mothers and fathers

Women who are expecting a baby have a legal right to time off work for antenatal care. They are also entitled to at least 26 weeks' maternity leave. These rights apply to full-time and part-time workers and it makes no difference how long the woman has worked for her employer. It is, however, important to follow the correct procedures and to give the employer enough notice about taking maternity leave. Some women may also be entitled to maternity pay but this depends on how long they have been working for their employer.

Fathers who have worked for their employer for at least 26 weeks are entitled to paternity leave, which provides up to two weeks' time off from work, with pay, when the child is born. It is important to tell your employer well in advance.

You can get advice and more information on maternity and paternity matters from the personnel officer at work, your trade union representative, your local Citizens Advice Bureau website **www.adviceguide.org.uk** or the government website **www.direct.gov.uk**.

### Childcare
It is Government policy to help people with childcare responsibilities to take up work. Some employers can help with this. The ChildcareLink website **www.childcarelink.gov.uk** gives information about different types of childcare and registered childminders in your area, or telephone 08000 96 02 96.

**6.14**  What is the minimum number of weeks' maternity leave that a woman in work is entitled to?
  **A**.  26 weeks
  **B**.  30 weeks
  **C**.  42 weeks
  **D**.  36 weeks

**6.15**  Which of the following statements is correct?
  **A**.  A father has to have been working for their employer for 26 weeks before he is entitled to paternity leave.
  **B**.  A father has to have been working for their employer for 40 weeks before he is entitled to paternity leave.

## Hours and time for children at work

In the UK there are strict laws to protect children from exploitation and to make sure that work does not get in the way of their education. The earliest legal age for children to do paid work is 13, although not all local authorities allow this. There are exceptions for some types of performance work (including modelling), when younger children may be allowed to work. Any child under school leaving age (16) seeking to do paid work must apply for a licence from the local authority. Children taking part in some kinds of performances may have to obtain a medical certificate before working.

By law, children under 16 can only do light work. There are particular jobs that children are not allowed to do. These include delivering milk, selling alcohol, cigarettes or medicines, working in a kitchen or behind the counter of a chip shop, working with dangerous machinery or chemicals, or doing any other kind of work that may be harmful to their health or education.

The law sets out clear limits for the working hours and times for 13–16-year-old children. Every child must have at least two consecutive weeks a year during the school holidays when they do not work. They cannot work:

■ for more than four hours without a one-hour rest break;
■ for more than two hours on any school day or a Sunday;

- more than five hours (13–14-year-olds) or eight hours (15–16-year-olds) on Saturdays (or weekdays during school holidays);
- before 7.00 a.m. or after 7.00 p.m.;
- before the close of school hours (except in areas where local bylaws allow children to work one hour before school);
- for more than 12 hours in any school week;
- for more than 25 hours a week (13–14-year-olds) or 35 hours a week (15–16-year-olds) during school holidays.

There is no national minimum wage for those under 16.

The local authority may withdraw a child's licence to work, for example where a child works longer hours than the law allows. The child would then be unable to continue to work. An employer may be prosecuted for illegally employing a child. A parent or carer who makes a false declaration in a child's licence application can also be prosecuted. They may also be prosecuted if they do not ensure their child receives a proper education. You can find more information on the TUC website: **www.worksmart.org.uk**.

---

### HELPING YOU LEARN

**6.16** Is the following statement TRUE or FALSE?
Children are allowed to deliver newspapers at 6:30 a.m.

**6.17** Look again at the study material and in Figure 6.6 add THREE more jobs that children are not allowed to do.

**Jobs children are not allowed to do.**

Working with dangerous machinery or chemicals

......................................................................................................

......................................................................................................

......................................................................................................

**Figure 6.6**

| **checklist** – Childcare and children at work |
| --- |

Now you have read Section 5, can you remember the following?

◼ **Entitlement to maternity leave and pay for both part-time and full-time workers.**

◼ **Paternity leave entitlement.**

◼ **The importance of following the right procedures and providing sufficient notice.**

◼ **The minimum age for starting work.**

◼ **Jobs that children under 16 are not allowed to do.**

◼ **The maximum hours allowed.**

◼ **Licence and medical certificate requirements.**

◼ **The local authority's role in licensing and protecting children in employment.**

◼ **Parents' responsibilities to ensure that children work within the law and get a proper education.**

# SECTION 6 Revision questions and end of chapter checklist

Now you have finished reading the official study material, try to answer the following questions to see how much of Chapter 6 you can remember. If you are unsure of the answers, check your notes and refer back to the text before looking at the answers at the end of the book.

## Revision questions for Chapter 6

1. What is NARIC?

Answer_____

2. What is the maximum number of hours a 13–16-year-old can work in any school week?

Answer_____

3. What is the minimum wage in the UK for workers aged 22 and over?

Answer_____

4. Which government department is responsible for collecting taxes?

Answer_____

5. What is the earliest age children can legally work?

Answer_____

6. What is a CRB check?

Answer_____

7. What is CV short for?

Answer_____

8. What are the benefits of volunteering?

Answer_____

9. Within how many months of starting in a new job should your employer give you a written contract or statement?

Answer_____

10. Which allowance can most people claim if they become unemployed?

Answer_____

---

**End of Chapter 6 checklist**

Tick the boxes when you have completed the following:

■ **read the study material;**                                        ☐

■ **made short notes to help you with your revision;**                ☐

■ **made a note and checked words that you do not understand;**       ☐

■ completed the *Helping you learn* and revision
  questions and checked your answers;  ☐

■ gone back and read again the sections for the
  questions you got wrong.  ☐

Well done, you have now completed all five chapters of the official study
material published by The Home Office.

Before you try the practice tests you might want to read your notes
again for Chapters 2–6 to remind yourself of the key information.

## Answers to *Helping you learn* questions for Chapter 6

6.1  B
6.2  Local and national newspapers
     Local Jobcentre
     Employment agencies
     Supermarket notice boards and shop windows
     Company websites
6.3  Education
     Qualifications
     Previous employment
6.4  Details of what the job involves
     Details of the pay
     Details about holidays
6.5  True
6.6  A   £3.30 per hour
     B   £4.45 per hour
     C   £5.35 per hour
6.7  16
6.8  C
6.9  65
6.10 Improving pay
     Improving working conditions
6.11 False – British citizens are permitted to work in EEA countries
6.12 Trade union representative
     Law Centre
     Citizens Advice Bureau
6.13 B
6.14 A

6.15   A

6.16   False – children can deliver newspapers, but not before 7 a.m.

6.17   Delivering milk
       Selling alcohol, cigarettes or medicines
       Working in a kitchen
       Working behind the counter in a chip shop
       Doing work that may be harmful to their health or education

# CHAPTER 7

# Glossary

This glossary will help readers to understand the meaning of key words and key expressions in the ways in which they are used and the context in which they appear in this handbook.

When words may be difficult to understand, an example of use may follow the definition.

The word that is bracketed after an entry relates to the particular context in which the word is being defined, e.g. applicant (employment).

A slash/ separates different definitions.

The convention s/he is used to mean 'she or he'.

This glossary is reproduced, with permission, from the official government publication *Life in the United Kingdom: A Journey to Citizenship*, published by the Stationery Office on behalf of the Home Office. The definitions in this glossary do not represent the views, opinions or policy of the National Institute of Adult and Continuing Education (NIACE).

(* Marks definitions that are not in the official glossary.)

## A

**absent from work**   not at work, e.g. because of illness

**abusive**   unkind or violent – usually used to describe behaviour towards another person

**academic course**   a series of lessons in which a student learns by studying information that s/he reads in books (see **vocational course**)

**access (internet)**   connect to/connection

**accountant**   a person whose job is to keep business records, to work out how much money a person or business is making or losing, and how much business tax needs to be paid (see **business accounts**)

**addictive substance**   usually a type of drug that a person feels a strong need to take very often, and finds very difficult to stop using

**adultery**   sex between a married person and someone who is not their husband or wife

**afford**   have enough money to pay for something

**allegiance**   loyalty to something, e.g. to a leader, a faith, a country or a cultural tradition

**amphetamine**   a type of drug which is addictive, powerful and illegal (see **addictive substance**)

**anonymous information**   information which is given by somebody whose name is unknown

**antenatal care**   medical care given to a woman (and to her unborn baby) while she is pregnant

**applicant (employment)**   someone who has asked an employer to give them a particular job – people often apply for jobs by writing a letter or completing a form

**application letter**   a formal letter sent to an employer asking for (applying for) a job

**appointment (employment)**   choose someone to do a job and formally offer it to them

**arbitrary (law)**   not bound by rules or law, and sometimes thought to be unfair

**armed forces**   the army, navy and air force which defend a country in times of peace and war

**arrested (police)**   taken by the police to a police station and made to stay there to answer questions about illegal actions or activity

**assault**   the criminal act of using physical force against someone or of attacking someone, e.g. hitting someone

**assessment methods (education)**   ways to measure a student's abilities or skills, e.g. a teacher can assess a child's reading and writing skills using a variety of different methods

**asylum**   a place where people who are accused of crime in another country can live in safety

**asylum seekers**   people who leave their own country because they feel it is too dangerous for them to stay there (usually because of political reasons) and who then formally ask to stay in another country where it will be safer for them to live (see **refuge**)

# B

**ban**   officially forbid

**bank holiday**   a day when most people have an official day off work and when banks and most other businesses are closed – a bank holiday can also be called a public holiday

**betting shop**   a place where a person can try to win money by gambling on the results of horse racing, football matches etc.

**bid (money)**   offer to pay a price for something when the cost is not fixed – other interested buyers may join in the bidding and the item will be sold to the highest bidder (the person who makes the highest offer)

**binding legally**   an agreement to do something which, by law, cannot be changed or be withdrawn from

*****binge drinking**   drinking large amounts of alcohol to excess in a short period of time

**birth certificate**   an official document that states the name of a person, the place and date of his/her birth, and the names and occupations of his/her parents

**birth parent**   a mother or father who is the natural, biological parent of a child

**birth rate**   the number of babies born, expressed as a percentage of a population, in a particular year or place

**bishop**   a senior priest in a Christian religion who is the head of different churches in a specified area

**boom**   a sharp rise in something – very often in business activity

**breach of contract**   a situation arising when a person breaks a legal agreement to do or not to do something

**British Empire**   a large number of states under British colonial rule and which, at one time in history, accounted for one-quarter of the world's population; many of these states are now independent, the rest are collectively known as the Commonwealth of Nations

**broker (finance)**   a person whose job is to give advice and to help select the most suitable and best value service in areas such as insurance and mortgages; also called a financial adviser

**brutality**   behaviour towards another person that is cruel and violent and causes harm

**building society**   a kind of bank which can be used for saving money or for borrowing money from in order to buy a house (see **mortgage**)

**built-up area**   a place where there are a lot of buildings and not many open spaces, and where a lot of people live and/ or work

**bureaux de change**   places where people can exchange one currency for another, e.g. they can sell pounds to buy euros

**burglary**   the criminal act of entering and stealing something from a building (see **theft**)

**bursary**   money in the form of a grant that a university gives to a student so they can study at university

**business accounts**   an official record of the amount of money a business is making, and how much it is paying for services or equipment etc., which is used to calculate the amount of tax that must be paid to the government (see **accountant**)

**by-election**   election which is held when an MP resigns or dies and when a new MP needs to be elected to replace him/her in Parliament before the next general election

## C

**Cabinet (government)**   a group of senior ministers who are responsible for controlling government policy

**cable company**   a company that can supply customers with a telephone or cable television connection

**cannabis**   an illegal drug that is usually smoked

**captivity**   being held in prison; not being allowed to move freely

**carriageway**   a single carriageway is a road that is only wide enough for one lane of traffic and that is divided from another road that takes traffic going in the opposite direction; a dual carriageway is a road that is wide enough for two lanes of traffic and that is divided from another road that takes traffic in the opposite direction

**cast a vote (government)**   formally register one choice from a number of options so that a group decision can be made about the most popular outcome, e.g. so that the MP with the largest number of supporters is the one who is elected

**casualties (medical)**   people who are wounded, e.g. in an accident or in a war

**caution (employment, law)**   a formal warning about something

**cautious**   careful, not wanting to get into a dangerous situation

**census (government)**   an official count of the number of people who live in a country and possibly includes information about those people, e.g. age, race, marital status etc.

**charity, give to**   give money or take action to help people who are suffering from poverty, illness, starvation etc.

**charter (government)**   an official written statement which describes the rights and the responsibilities of a state and its citizens

**childminder**   a person whose job is to look after young children, usually while the children's parents are at work – a childminder usually has a qualification to do this kind of work

**circulate (money)**   pass from one person to another and then to another etc.

**civil disobedience**   the refusal of members of the public to obey laws, often because they want to protest against political issues

**Civil Service**   the departments within government which manage the business of running the country – people who work for the government can be called civil servants

**clarification (language)**   a clear way to say something that is easy to understand

**clergy**   Christian church officials, e.g. priests and bishops

**coalition**   a partnership between political parties

**cocaine**   a type of drug which is addictive, powerful and illegal; it can be used by doctors to control pain (see **addictive substance**)

**code of practice**   an agreed set of professional rules and procedures that someone in work is expected to follow

**colleagues**   people who work together in the same company and who often have professional jobs

**commemorate**   do something to show that something or someone is remembered, usually on a particular day

**commit a crime**   do something which is against the law (see **criminal**; **criminal offence**)

**Commonwealth of Nations**   an association of Britain and of sovereign states that used to be British colonies or states that are still ruled by Britain – the British monarch is accepted by the Commonwealth countries as their ruler

**community events**   events which are organised within a local area to help, in some way, the people who live or work in the same area, e.g. a town might hold a community event in order to raise money to buy special equipment for a local school

**compensation (money)**   money which must be paid to someone because they have suffered in some way, e.g. loss, injury; compensation

can also be paid to a person if their employer has treated them unfairly
or illegally

**compulsory testing**   tests that must be done by law

**concern**   worry about an important problem/a worrying thing

**concession**   a right that is given to someone to end an argument or
disagreement

**confidential information**   information that is private and secret, and
only known to the giver and receiver of that information

**consecutive**   following one another without a break or interruption, e.g.
next week we must have meetings on two consecutive days, Tuesday
and Wednesday

**constituency**   a specific area where the voters who live in that place (its
constituents) can elect an MP to represent them in Parliament

**constitution (law)**   the legal structure of established laws and principles
which is used to govern a country

**consumer problem**   a problem people have that is to do with things
they have bought or services they have paid for

**contraception**   method used to prevent women who have sex from
becoming pregnant, e.g. taking contraceptive pills, using a condom

**contributions (finance)**   money paid regularly by someone which will
help pay for something which is worth much more, e.g. a pension

**convention (government)**   an official agreement, usually between
countries, about particular rules or codes of behaviour

**corrupt (behaviour)**   acting in a dishonest and illegal way

**coverage (media)**   newspaper reports that can be read in the press (see
**free press**)

**credit card**   a card that a person can use to buy goods or services that
are paid for by a credit company – the credit company then sends the
cardholder a monthly bill; goods can therefore be bought, but paid for
later (see **debit card**)

**criminal**   a person who is found guilty of breaking the law

**criminal offence**   an illegal activity, e.g. burglary, for which the criminal
may be prosecuted

**currency (money)**   a particular system of money that a country or
group of countries can use, e.g. in the EU, the form of currency that is
used most widely is the euro

**cut off (services)**   disconnect the supply of something


**D**

**debate**   a discussion in which people give different opinions about
something; to discuss and give different opinions about something

**debit card**  a card that a person can use to buy goods or services with money that is in their bank or building society account – the money is taken from the account automatically (see **credit card**)

**decline in numbers**  reduce, decrease, fall, go down

**decree (law)**  official order, law or decision

**defeat**  to be stronger than an opponent and therefore win a battle, a war, a competition etc.

**defer**  delay until a later time

**degrading (treatment)**  treatment that causes humiliation (see **humiliated**)

**democratic country**  a county which is governed by people who are elected by the population to represent them in Parliament

**deport**  make someone leave a country and, usually, return to the country from which they originally came – this is because the person who must be deported does not have the legal right to stay

**deposit (housing)**  an amount of money paid to the landlord when a person rents a flat or house – this money is given back when the person leaves, but only if the property or furniture has not been damaged

**deposit (money)**  an amount of money that is not the full price of something – the rest, 'the balance', must be paid later

**descent, of**  coming originally from, e.g. of Indian descent means being a member of a family coming originally from India (see **roots**; **ethnic origin**)

**devolution**  the passing of power from a central government to another group at a regional or local level, which can then be called a devolved administration

**dialect**  a form of language which is spoken only by a particular social group or by a group of people living in a particular area

**direct debit**  an arrangement that a person makes to transfer an amount of money from his/her bank account into another account on a regular basis (see **standing order**)

**disability, physical/mental**  a condition that a person has that makes doing ordinary things like walking, seeing, speaking, talking or learning difficult

**discrimination**  the act of treating an individual or a particular group of people in a way which is unfair, for example because of their race, nationality, sex, sexuality, age or disability; paying a woman less than a man for the same work is an example of discrimination

**dismissal (employment)**  removal from the job, the 'sack'

**disputes**  arguments or disagreements that are serious and about which people may take legal advice or action

**divorce**   the legal end of a marriage; the act of ending a marriage

**domestic policies**   political decisions that relate to what is happening within a country (as opposed to in another country)

**domestic rates**   a type of tax in Northern Ireland which is paid by residents to their local authorities and which helps to pay for local services, e.g. education, road repairs, policing, refuse collection

**domestic violence**   fighting or acting aggressively in the home and causing mental or physical harm to someone in the family

**dominion**   a country that was once colonised but that is now self-governing

**dump**   get rid of something, throw away – often in a place where rubbish should not be left; a place where rubbish is left in an untidy and unhealthy way

**dwelling**   a place where people live, e.g. a house, a flat


**E**

**ecstasy**   a type of drug which is illegal and dangerous – it makes users feel that they have lots of energy, but can cause death (see **addictive substance**)

**elect a person**   choose someone by voting for them

**electoral register**   the official list of all the people in the country who are allowed to vote in an election

**electorate**   all the people who are allowed to vote in an election

**eligible**   allowed by law

**emergency services**   services that can be telephoned and that will come to the help of people when they need it quickly and very urgently, e.g. the police service, the fire service, the ambulance service, the coastguard service and, at sea, the lifeguard service

**employ**   give someone work and pay them to do it

**employee**   someone who is paid by an employer to do a job

**employer**   a person or company that gives work to other people and pays them for doing it

**engagement (family)**   an agreement between two people that they will get married at some time in the future – these people are engaged to one another but not married yet (see **fiancé**; **fiancée**)

**enterprise (business)**   business energy – the starting and running of business activities

**\*ESOL**   English for Speakers of other Languages

**ethnic minority**   a group of people who are of a different race from the race of the majority of the population in a particular country

**ethnic origin**   the country of birth, someone's race or the nationality of someone when they were born; the customs and place from which a person and their family originate (see **roots**)

**European Union (or EU)**   a political and economical association of European countries which encourages trade and cooperation between its member states

**evict (housing)**   order someone legally to leave the house where they are living

**evidence, collecting**   looking for and getting information, documents or items that show for certain that something has happened, e.g. the police went to the criminal's house to collect as much evidence as possible (see **proof**)

**exchange rate**   the amount of money in one currency that you need to buy a certain amount of money in another currency, e.g. £1 = $1.9 (see **bureaux de change**); this exchange rate can vary from day to day

**exiled**   sent to another country and not allowed to return as an act of political punishment

**expel**   force someone officially to leave an organisation of some kind

**exploitation**   a situation in which someone is made to do something unfairly because they are given nothing or very little for doing it, e.g. the women were exploited by their employer, who paid them less than the minimum wage and also forced them to work overtime

**expression, freedom of**   talking about personal ideas or beliefs without getting into any legal trouble for doing so

**F**

**facilities in the community**   local services that the public can use, e.g. libraries, schools, hospitals

**famine**   a situation in which there is very little food for a long time and people often die because of this

**fiancé**   a man who has formally agreed to marry a woman

**fiancée**   a woman who has formally agreed to marry a man (see **engagement**)

**first past the post**   a system of election in which the candidate with the largest number of voters in a particular consistency wins a seat in Parliament

**flooding (housing)**   water coming inside a property (and which probably causes damage to it)

**free press**   newspaper and other reporting media that are not controlled by government and can therefore write freely, without restriction, about anything they think their readers will be interested in

## G

**gambling (money)**   risking money to win more money, e.g. in card games or by trying to guess the winner of a horse race or football match

**gap year (education)**   a year between leaving school and going to university during which many students choose to gain experience through travelling, or to earn money by taking a job

**general election**   a situation in which all the citizens of a country who are allowed to vote choose the people they wish to represent them in their government – in Britain this usually happens every five years (see **MP**)

**government policies**   official ideas and beliefs that are agreed by a political party about how to govern the country (see **party politics**)

**grant (money)**   an amount of money paid by an authority to help a person or organisation pay for a particular thing, e.g. an education course, a business expansion

## H

**hard drugs**   drugs which are illegal and are very powerful and addictive

**harassment (behaviour)**   rude, offensive, threatening or bullying behaviour – a word often used to describe this kind of behaviour in a workplace

**health authority, local**   an organisation which manages healthcare and from which people can get advice about where to find medical help

**health hazard**   things that might be dangerous to someone's health, e.g. smoking is a hazard to health because it can cause lung cancer

**heir**   someone who will legally receive another person's money, property, possessions or position when that person dies

**helmet**   a hard hat that protects the head against injury – a crash helmet must be worn by someone who is riding a motorcycle

**heroin**   a type of drug which is addictive, powerful and illegal (see **addictive substance**)

**higher education**   education that students receive at college or university

**holding public office**   having a job in one of the services or industries that are managed by the government

**House of Commons**   the part of the Houses of Parliament where MPs who are elected by the voting public debate political issues

**House of Lords**   the part of the Houses of Parliament where the people who have inherited seats or been especially chosen by the Prime Minister debate political issues

**Houses of Parliament**   the building in London which comprises the House of Commons, the House of Lords and other offices where the British Parliament meets, debates and passes laws

**household**   the home and the people who live in it; something that relates to the home, e.g. household chores are jobs that need to be done in the home, like cleaning and cooking

**humiliated**   feeling ashamed, stupid, embarrassed because of something that happens to you, usually when other people are there

**I**

**immigration**   enter another country to live and work there – someone who does this is an immigrant (see **migrate**)

**inappropriate touching**   touching someone on part of his/her body in a way that is offensive and not acceptable in a particular situation

**indecent remark**   something that is said that contains words which are rude, sexual and offensive

**independents (politics)**   MPs who do not represent any of the main political parties

**inflation (money)**   the rate at which prices rise over a period of time

**infrastructure**   structured network that is necessary for the successful operation of a business or transport system, e.g. roads or railways

**inheritance**   a sum of money, possessions or property that someone has the legal right to receive after the death of (usually) a relative, e.g. a son might inherit his father's fortune

**inhuman (behaviour)**   very harsh, cruel and degrading

**in-patient**   someone who needs medical care and needs to stay in hospital overnight or longer

**instalments (money)**   a series of equal payments which are paid regularly over a period of time until the total cost of something is paid, e.g. a person may pay for a TV that costs £200 in ten monthly instalments of £20

**insulting words**   rude words which also make people feel very unhappy, worried or stupid

**insure**   pay money to an insurance company in case, e.g., a car or property is damaged – if this happens, the insurance company will pay for repairs

**intentionally**   on purpose, deliberately

**interest (money)**   extra money that must be paid to a lender when someone borrows money – this is usually calculated as a percentage of the loan – if the interest rate is 10 per cent and the person borrows £100, the interest that must be paid on the loan will be an extra £10

**internet café**   a place where people can go and pay to use a computer to look up information on websites or to send emails – the cost depends on how long they want to use a computer for, e.g. 30 minutes

**interpreter**   a person whose job is to change something that is spoken or written in one language into another language without changing the meaning

**irretrievably broken down**   when there is no hope of solving problems and making a bad situation better again

**Islamic mortgage**   a loan for buying a house, when the person who receives the loan only needs to pay back the original sum – no extra money needs to be paid

**J**

**judge (law)**   the most important official in court whose job is to make sure that court proceedings are lawful and fair, and to decide which punishment to give a criminal if s/he is found guilty by the court

**judiciary**   all the judges in a country who, together, are responsible for using the law of the land in the correct way

**jury**   ordinary people (usually a group of 12 people) who listen to information and then decide whether someone is guilty or innocent in a court of law

**L**

**labour (employment)**   work which is often physical; workers

**landlord, landlady (housing)**   a man (landlord) or woman (landlady) who owns a house or flat and rents it to people (tenants) who must pay them money (rent) to live there

**landlord, landlady (pub)**   the owner or manager of a pub

**lane (transport)**   part of a road, usually marked by white lines, which is only wide enough for one vehicle to travel in (see **carriageway**)

**legal**   allowed to do by law or must do by law

**legal aid**   money that a person can ask for to help them pay for the services of a solicitor and, if necessary, court costs

**legal procedure**   the way that something is done by law

**legislative power**   the power to make laws

**legitimate children**   children whose parents are married to each other when they are born

**leisure centre**   a building where people can go and pay to do sports indoors, e.g. swimming, badminton

**letting agent**   a service which helps landlords find tenants and tenants find places to rent (see **landlord, landlady (housing)**)

**liberty**   freedom

**lock**   close something securely, usually with a key, so that other people cannot easily open it

**long standing**   having already existed for a long time

**L plates**   a sign on a car to show that the driver is still learning to drive and has not yet passed their driving test – an L plate is a red 'L' in a white square


**M**

**magistrate**   a person who acts as a judge in a court case where the crime is not as serious as some others

**mainland**   an area of land which forms a country and does not include any of its surrounding islands

**manufacturer**   the maker of a product which is sold to the public

**marital status**   information about whether a person is single, married, separated or divorced that is often asked for on official forms

**maternity leave**   time allowed off work for a woman during her pregnancy and after her baby is born and during which time she usually continues to receive a wage (see **paternity leave**)

**maternity services**   medical and social help relating to motherhood from early pregnancy until after the baby has been born

**media**   all the organisations that give information to the public, e.g. newspapers, magazines, television, radio and the internet

**mediation**   advice and support given by a person or organisation to end an argument between two other people or groups of people who cannot agree about something

**medical consultation**   speaking to a doctor and getting information and advice, e.g. about health issues, illness

**mental illness**   an illness in which a person appears to behave or think in ways that are not considered to be normal, e.g. 'depression' is a mental illness that makes people feel unnecessarily sad, worried or frightened and can prevent them from doing routine things like shopping, having fun with friends etc.

**meter (housing)**   a machine that shows, in units or numbers, how much electricity, gas or water has been used in a household

**meter reading (housing)**   the number on a meter that shows how much electricity, gas or water has been used

**migrate (people)**   move to another country to live and work there – someone who does this is a migrant (see **immigration**)

**military service, compulsory**   every adult (usually male) must join the armed forces for a particular period of time – this is not required by law in the UK

**misuse**   use something in a wrong way or for a wrong reason

**molestation**   a sexual attack on someone (often a child)

**monarch**   the king or queen of a country

**mortgage**   a loan, usually from a building society or bank, that is used to buy or help buy a house or flat – the loan is usually paid back in instalments over a number of years (see **building society**)

**motor (transport)**   a machine that makes something move; a car

**MP**   Member of Parliament – the person who is elected by his or her constituents to represent them in government

**N**

**national issues**   political problems that affect everyone who lives in a country

**nationalised**   bought and then controlled by central government – relating to an industry or service that was previously owned privately (see **privatised**)

**naturalised citizen**   someone who is born in one country but becomes a citizen of another country

**not-for-profit**   a way of doing business in which an organisation or company will not try to make money from providing their service or goods

**notice, to give**   to give someone information about something that is going to happen in the future that will change a situation

**notice (employment)**   a length of time that an employee must continue to work after telling an employer that s/he wants to leave the job; a length of time that an employer must continue to employ someone after asking her/him to leave, e.g. my boss only gave me one week's notice, so I was really upset

**nuisance (behaviour)**   something that annoys or causes problems for other people

**O**

**obstructive behaviour**   being difficult and stopping someone from doing something, or stopping something from happening on purpose

**occupation (employment)**   job

**offensive (behaviour)**   rude and upsetting

**office, to be in**   to be in power in government

**off-licence**   a shop that sells alcohol in bottles or cans, e.g. wine, beer

**online**   on the internet

**Opposition**   the second largest party that is not in power in government, e.g. in 2006, the Labour Party was in power and the Conservatives were in Opposition, and David Cameron was Leader of the Opposition

**outpatient**   someone who receives medical care in a hospital but does not need to stay overnight


**P**

**packaging**   material, e.g. boxes, see-through plastic, that covers and protects things that are for sale, e.g. food

**party politics**   the shared and particular ideas and beliefs of an organised group of politicians, e.g. the Labour Party

**paternity leave**   time allowed off work for a man whose wife or partner is going to have a baby or has just had a baby and during which time he continues to receive a wage (see **maternity leave**)

**patient (medical)**   someone whom a doctor looks after or who needs medical care because they are ill, have an injury etc.

**patriarchy**   a system of society in which men hold all the power and in which power can be passed from father to son

**patriotism**   the pride of belonging to, and love of, a country

**patron saint**   a Christian saint who, according to religious belief, protects a particular place or a particular group of people

**peers**   members of the House of Lords

**penalty (law)**   punishment for breaking the law, e.g. a fine

**pension plan, pay into a**   to save money regularly while a person is working so that, when a person stops going to work at 60 or older, there will be enough money to provide him/her with a pension (see **State Pension**)

**performing (theatre)**   acting or dancing

**persecuted**   hunted and punished, perhaps even killed, e.g. someone might be persecuted for holding a particular religious belief

**personal details**   information about a person that can be used to identify them, e.g. their name, date of birth, address, marital status etc.

**personnel officer**   someone whose job in a company is to employ staff and to help solve problems that employees have at work

**phonecard, pre-paid**   a card that can be bought and then used to make a certain number of phone calls up to the value of the card

**PIN number**   four numbers which have to be tapped into a cash machine if someone wants to withdraw money from their account or pay for something using a credit or debit card; using a Personal Identification Number (PIN) stops other people from using cards if they are stolen, so the numbers must be remembered and kept secret

**places of worship**   religious buildings like churches or mosques where people can go to practise their religion, e.g. to pray or sing

**pocket money**   a small amount of money that a parent might give to his/her child on a regular basis, e.g. once a week, so that the child can buy his/her own comics or sweets etc.

**pogrom**   the intentional killing of many people usually because of their race or religious belief

**pooled savings**   amounts of money that have been saved by different people and added together to make a larger sum of jointly owned money

**Pope, the**   the leader of the Roman Catholic Church

**possessions**   things that people own, e.g. a car, clothes, a television, books

**practise a religion**   actively live according to the rules, customs and beliefs of that religion, e.g. go to church, take part in prayer, wear special clothing etc.

**pregnancy**   the nine-month period before birth during which a baby grows inside its mother – the mother is pregnant at this time

**prehistoric**   a time in history before any records were written down

**prescription (medical)**   a note from a doctor saying which medicines a patient needs

**pressure group**   a group of people who try to persuade the government to do something or to persuade the public to change their opinion about something

**Prime Minister**   the Member of Parliament who is the leader of the political party in power and therefore of the whole government

**privatised**   bought and then controlled by the private sector – relating to an industry or service that was previously owned by the government (see **nationalised**)

**prohibit**   to say something is illegal; stop someone doing something; make something illegal or forbid something

**promotion (employment)**   movement to a better or more important job within the same company, e.g. she was promoted from shop assistant to sales manageress

**proof**   information, items, documents etc. that show that something has definitely happened (see **evidence, collecting**)

**proportional representation**  a system of election in which political parties are allowed a number of seats in Parliament that represents their share of the number of votes cast

**prosperity**  a time of wealth or increase in fortune

**provinces**  areas into which a country is divided for governmental reasons

**pub**  public house – a place where adults over the age of 18 can buy and drink alcohol

**public, a member of the**  a person who is an ordinary member of the community and not a government official

**public body**  a governmental department or a group of people who represent or work for the government and work for the good of the general public

**public place**  a place which is not private and where ordinary people can spend time together, or on their own, e.g. a cinema, a restaurant, a library, a pub, a park

**punctual**  arriving at the right time, not being late for something, e.g. work or a doctor's appointment

**R**

**racial**  relating to race, e.g. racial discrimination (see **discrimination**)

**racism**  aggressive behaviour towards (or treatment of) people who come from a different race by people who wish to be unkind and unfair to them

**raising (family)**  looking after children as they grow so that they are safe and healthy

**receipt (money)**  a piece of paper with a description of something that has been bought and its price – given by a shop to a customer as a record of the purchase

**recruit (employment)**  find people and offer them work in a company or business

**recycle rubbish**  separate rubbish into different materials, e.g. put all the paper in one place and all the glass in another, so that each material can be processed in a separate way and used again, e.g. broken glass can be made into new bottles

**redundant (employment)**  no longer needed to do a particular job, e.g. if a person is made redundant, there is no longer a job for that person to do in a particular company and they will be asked to leave – if this happens the employee may be entitled to receive an amount of money (**redundancy** pay)

**referendum** a vote by the public or by a governing body to decide on a course of action to make a political decision

**Reformation, the** the religious movement in the sixteenth century that challenged the authority of the Pope and established Protestant churches in Europe – Protestant comes from the word 'protest'

**refuge** a place where a person can stay and be kept safe from danger

**refugees** people who must leave the country where they live, often because of war or political reasons (see **asylum seekers**)

**refund (money)** give a customer an amount of money back that is equal to the price of something s/he bought but returned to the shop, e.g. because the item does not work properly

**rent (housing)** pay to live in a room, flat or house that is owned by someone else

**residence** the place where someone lives; their address

**residential trips (school)** visits to places when students stay away from home for one night or longer and have to sleep in other accommodation

**resign (employment)** decide officially to leave a certain job

**restrict (immigration)** control and/or limit the number of people, e.g. a government might restrict the number of immigrants who can come and live in a country

**retail work** jobs that involve working in shops and selling goods to customers

**retire (employment)** stop going to work, usually at the age of 65 or older

**rise (in number, price)** increase, go up

**rival viewpoints** opinions that are held by different people or groups of people that are in opposition to each other

**roots (family)** the place that someone relates to because that was where s/he was born or where his/her family had their established home

**S**

**scratch card** a card that a person buys and then rubs with a coin to see if they have won money (see **gambling**)

**scrutinise** examine all the details

**seat (government)** a position that is officially held by someone in government who has been elected by the public and authorised to represent them

**second-hand goods**   something that someone else has already owned

**security**   protection from something that could be dangerous, e.g. a person or thing that is secure is safe and protected from danger

**self-employed person**   someone who works for themselves and not for an employer

**sentence (law)**   length of time that a criminal must stay in prison as a punishment for the crime s/he has committed – this is decided by a judge at the end of a court case

**separation (family)**   a situation where a married couple no longer live together but are not yet divorced

**serious misconduct (employment)**   behaviour by someone in a job which is dishonest, bad or unprofessional, and because of which they may lose their job

**Shadow Cabinet**   a group of senior MPs with special responsibilities who belong to a party that is not in government (which can also be called the **Opposition**)

**sick pay**   money received by an employee when s/he is unable to work because of illness

**signatory**   a person who signs their name (puts their signature) on an official document – e.g. to show their agreement to an official arrangement

**solicitor**   a professional person whose job is to give legal advice and prepare documents for legal procedures, e.g. divorce, buying and selling houses

**Speaker, the**   the person in government who controls the way issues are debated in Parliament

**stand for office**   apply to be elected as an MP or local councillor

**standing order**   an arrangement in which a bank or building society takes a fixed amount of money from one account and pays it into another account on a regular basis (see **direct debit**)

**start-up loan**   money given to someone to start up a new business that must be paid back with interest later

**State Pension**   money paid regularly by the government to people who have retired from work, usually when they are 65 or older

**stepfamily**   a family in which the mother or father is not the biological parent of one or more of the children, e.g. when a divorced woman remarries, her new husband will be the stepfather to the children from her previous marriage

**strike, to go on**   refuse to work in order to protest against something, e.g. low wages, long hours

**successor (government)**    a person who comes after another and who will often receive some kind of power when that happens, e.g. a son who becomes king when his father, the old king, dies is the successor to the throne

**surveyor (housing)**    a person who examines a property (usually when it is for sale) and checks the condition of the building; s/he then writes an official report (a survey), which gives important information to the buyer about any problems, or about any repairs that might need to be done

**suspend**    to officially stop, usually for a short time, something from happening or operating

**T**

**taster session (training)**    an introductory part of a course that allows someone to try it and to see if it is what they would like to do

**tenancy**    the period of time that a tenant rents a property from a landlord or landlady – often also relating to conditions about renting the property

**tenant**    a person who pays money to a landlord or landlady to live in rented accommodation – a flat or a house

**terrorism**    violence used by people who want to force governments to do something – the violence is usually random and unexpected so no one can feel really safe from it

**theft**    the criminal act of stealing something from a person, building or place (see **burglary**)

**therapist (psychology)**    a professional person whose job it is to help people to understand why they have problems and to help them solve their problems

**timescale**    the planned length of time it takes to complete something, usually at work

**toddler (family)**    a small child, usually 1–2 years old – the age at which children learn to walk

**torture**    hurt someone in a very cruel way and on purpose, e.g. to try to make them give information or to punish them

**trade union**    an association of workers that protects its members' political rights

**trader**    someone who trades – who buys and sells goods

**treaty**    an official written agreement between countries or governments

**tuition fees**    money paid to a teacher or a school for being taught something

# U

**unemployed**   not doing a job and not getting any wages

**uprising**   a violent revolt or rebellion against an authority

**utilities, public**   services that the public can use, e.g. the supply of water, gas or electricity

# V

**vacancy (employment)**   a job that is available and that an employer needs someone to do

**valid**   legally acceptable, e.g. when someone wants to enter another country his/her passport must be valid for that to be allowed

**vehicle (transport)**   something in which people can travel on the roads, e.g. a car or bus

**vetoed, to be vetoed**   officially refused permission to do something, often by an organisation

**victim**   someone who is hurt or harmed by something that another person has done

**vocational course**   a series of lessons in which a student is taught the practical skills that are necessary to do a certain job, e.g. to become a plumber or car mechanic (see **academic course**)

**voluntarily**   in a willing way, e.g. a person who does something voluntarily does it because they want to, and not because someone has asked them to do it or because someone has said they must do it

**voluntary work**   work which someone does because they want to and which they do for free, i.e. they do not receive any payment (see **volunteer**)

**volunteer**   someone who works for free or who offers to do something without payment (see **voluntary work**)

**vulnerable people**   people who can be easily hurt or harmed, e.g. because of their age

# W

**wages (pay)**   an amount of money paid for work

**war effort**   the work that people did in order to support the country in whatever way they could during wartime

**welfare benefits**   amounts of money paid by the government to people who have very little money of their own and who are perhaps unable to work or elderly or sick or disabled etc.

**withdraw (money)**   take money out of a bank account or cash machine

**workforce**   the group of people who work for a particular company or business or, on a large scale, all the people who can work in a particular country or part of the world etc.

**working days**   the days on which, typically, most people go to work – in the UK these are Monday, Tuesday, Wednesday, Thursday and Friday

## Y

**Yellow Pages**   a book that lists names, addresses and telephone numbers of businesses, services and organisations in an area

# CHAPTER 8

# Taking the test

This chapter gives you important information about the process of booking the test, what to expect on the day of the test and what happens after you have taken the test.

The chapter includes examples of the four types of questions that are used in the test.

## IMPORTANT INFORMATION

Remember, if you are taking the test in Northern Ireland, Wales or Scotland, make sure you read and remember the information about the country where you live as some of the questions are likely to be specific to your country.

This chapter is divided into four sections.

**Section 1** Booking the test.

**Section 2** What to expect on the day of the test.

**Section 3** Tips to help you when you take the test.

**Section 4** What happens after the test?

# SECTION 1   Booking the test

### Can I take the test close to where I live?

You can take the test at one of the many test centres that are around the UK. You can find out where your nearest test centre is by looking at the official government *Life in the UK* test website **www.lifeintheuktest.gov.uk**. You can also call the Helpline on 0800 0154245.

### I want to arrange to take the test; what do I do?

You can book a test by phoning a test centre during opening hours or by visiting the centre. You will have to wait at least seven days before you can take the test.

### What happens if I need to change the date of my test?

You need to tell the test centre as soon as possible if you want to change the date of the test. Some centres may charge a £10 fee if you tell them less than seven days before the test date.

### How much will the test cost?

The test costs £33.28 (VAT inclusive); you will need to pay this fee before taking the test.

### What identification do I need to take with me when I take the test?

It's important to take photographic identification with you. Make sure that all the photographs on the documents look like you; if they don't they may not be accepted.

Remember to take one of the following forms of photographic ID with you:

- a passport (from your country of origin);

- one of the following Home Office travel documents:

    - a Convention Travel Document;

    - a Certificate of Identity Document;

    - a Stateless Person Document;

- a UK photocard driving licence, full or provisional;

- an Immigration Status Document, endorsed with a UK Residence Permit showing a photograph of the holder (which must be together on the same document).

If you have any letters from the Home Office, they will contain a reference number and your postcode. You need to take these with you when you take the test.

If you haven't had any letters from the Home Office you will need to take proof of your postcode, for example an electricity or gas bill or a bank statement.

If you are unsure which documents to take with you, check by phoning the Helpline on 0800 0154245.

### What do I do if I have a disability and need special support to take the test?

If you have a disability it's important to tell the test supervisor about your particular requirements when you book the test. People with some disabilities do not have to take the test at all.

The test is available in three different formats, so you can choose to take your test in the format that best suits you. To find out more about this, ask when you book your test. Examples of the different styles are on the *Life in the UK* test website: **www.lifeintheuktest.gov.uk**.

### Is the test only available in English?

The test is in English. If you are taking the test in Scotland or Wales you can ask to take the test in Scottish Gaelic or in the Welsh language. If you want to do this you will need to contact your test centre.

### I haven't used a computer before; can I take a written test?

You will need to take the test on a computer at an official test centre but don't worry if you haven't used a computer before. You only need very basic computer skills.

Just make sure you practise using a keyboard and a mouse before you take the test. If you have a computer there is mouse and keyboard training available on the **www.lifeintheuktest.gov.uk**.

If you do not have access to a computer, don't worry. There are lots of places where you can access computers, for example at your local library or at one of the UK online centres in England. They will give you advice on how to use the computers. You could ask a friend to check the website **www.ukonlinecentres.com** to locate your nearest centre.

You could also go to your local Learndirect centre. To find your nearest centre phone, in England, 0800 101901 or, in Scotland, 0808 100 9000.

If you live in Wales or Northern Ireland you could go to your local library as most of them will have computers available.

# SECTION 2 What to expect on the day of the test

**Can I take children and friends with me?**
You cannot take children and friends into the test room and there may not be a waiting area for them.

**What information will I be asked for at the test centre?**
The test supervisor will ask you for the following information, which they will check and record:

 your full name;

■ date of birth;

■ nationality;

■ postcode;

■ country and place of birth;

■ Home Office reference.

The test supervisor will also check your photographic ID.

**What will I be tested on?**
The test is based on the Home Office handbook *Life in the United Kingdom: A Journey to Citizenship*. It is computer-based and there are 24 multiple-choice questions.

**Can I take a practice test at the test centre?**
When the test supervisor has logged you on to a computer you will have the opportunity to complete a practice test before you start the *Life in the UK* test.

**I prefer to listen to the questions; is this possible?**
When you take the test you can select to listen to the questions.

**If I live in Scotland, Wales or Northern Ireland will there be questions about my country?**
The test will include questions that ask you about the part of the UK where you live.

**How long do I have to complete the test?**
You will have 45 minutes to answer 24 questions.

It is very important that you do not rush to finish the test. You will have enough time to choose your answers carefully and to check them.

If you have certain medical conditions you may be allowed more time to complete the test. You must tell the test centre this information when you book your test.

### Does the test have a pass mark?
The pass mark is 75%. This means you will need to get at least 18 answers correct.

### Will I take the test by myself?
There are usually about 15 other people taking the test at the same time.

### Can I take books, notes or other equipment into the test with me?
You cannot take any books or notes with you and you will not be able to use any electronic devices such as a mobile phone.

### What types of multiple-choice questions are in the test?
The test contains four different types of questions.

### Question type 1
The first type of question involves choosing **one** correct answer from four options. The following question is an example. It is not a real test question.

---

Children in the UK must attend school until they are:

☐ 13 years old

☐ 18 years old

☐ 16 years old

☐ 17 years old

---

The correct answer is 16 years old.

In this type of question you need to select one answer only and click on the white circle next to your chosen answer. When you have clicked on the circle it will be filled with a small dot to show that it has been selected.

## Question type 2

In this type of question you will need to decide whether a statement is **true** or **false.** You will need to select the correct answer. Remember the example below isn't a real test question.

> Is the statement below TRUE or FALSE?
>
> In Britain there are more people over 60 than children under 16.
>
> ☐ TRUE
>
> ☐ FALSE

The statement is TRUE.

## Question type 3

When you see this type of question you will need to choose two correct answers from the four options.

With this type of question it is very important to make sure that you have selected two answers.

> In which TWO places can you find the name of a dentist?
>
> ☐ By calling your local authority
>
> ☐ By asking at a Citizens Advice Bureau
>
> ☐ By calling NHS Direct
>
> ☐ By asking your doctor

The correct answers are 'By calling NHS Direct' and 'By asking at a Citizens Advice Bureau'.

## Question type 4

In the last type of question you will need to choose which one of the two statements is correct.

Again, remember the example below isn't a real test question.

> Which of these statements is correct?
>
> ☐ The Scouse dialect is spoken in Liverpool
>
> ☐ The Scouse dialect is spoken in Manchester

The correct answer is 'The Scouse dialect is spoken in Liverpool'.

### How do I know how much time I have left to complete the questions?

There is a timer on the computer screen that will count down and show you the amount of time you have left. You will have a time alert when you are halfway through the test time and again when you have ten minutes and two minutes left to complete the test. It is important that you plan your time so that you do not rush the test.

### What happens if I want to change or check my answer?

On each question screen there are boxes at the top of the screen showing which questions you have answered. If you want to change your answer to a previous question, you return to them by clicking 'Previous Question' at the bottom of the screen.

### What happens if I run out of time?

The test will automatically end and you will not be allowed to finish the current question. But remember, most people have plenty of time so use the timer to check your progress and don't rush.

# SECTION 3  Tips to help you when you take the test

The following tips will help you when you take the test. Remember, the most important thing is to stay calm and relaxed as you won't be able to concentrate if you get stressed. Also remember, if you do fail the test you can take it again as often as you need to.

## Getting the basics right

Make sure you get enough sleep before the day of the test and plan to have something to eat and drink so that you are not hungry or thirsty.

Remember, if you do not have enough to drink your brain does not work as effectively.

Plan your journey in advance to make sure you arrive in plenty of time for the test and do not feel rushed.

Check carefully that your personal details are entered correctly on to the test system. It is your responsibility to ensure that they are correct.

Make sure you listen to the test supervisor carefully and ask if there is anything you don't understand.

## Answering the questions

Take advantage of the practice test that you will be offered by the test supervisor. This will give you an opportunity to practice using the computer. You will also be able to see what the test looks like on the screen.

Remember that you can switch on the audio for the test if you prefer to hear the questions read out loud.

If you want to make notes during the test you could ask the test supervisor for blank paper and a pen.

Read the questions carefully and make sure you understand what you have to do.

Plan your time – 45 minutes gives you just under 2 minutes per question. This should give you plenty of time to answer the questions and check them.

---

DID YOU KNOW?

**Did you know that most people complete the test in 22 minutes? Don't forget that you have 45 minutes, so don't rush.**

---

Use the timer on the test screen to help you plan your time.

Answer every question even if you are not sure if you have chosen the correct answer. It's much better to guess an answer than to leave the question unanswered, as you may have guessed the correct answer. If there are only two possible answers you have a 50/50 chance of getting it right.

If you don't know the answer to one of the questions, see if you can identify if any of the options are obviously wrong. This will help to narrow down your choice of possible correct answers.

Remember not to spend too much time on any one question – you can always make a note of it and go back to it later.

# SECTION 4  What happens after the test?

### How long do I need to wait to get the result of the test?

You will not have to wait long to find out your result. The test supervisor will let you know whether you have passed the test while you are still at the centre.

### What happens next if I pass the test?

You will be given a pass notification letter that you will need to sign before you leave the centre.

## **IMPORTANT** INFORMATION

It is very important that you keep your letter in a safe place as it cannot be replaced. If you lose it you may have to pay to take the test again.

### What happens if I fail the test?

If you fail the test, don't worry. You can retake the test as many times as you want.

You'll have to wait a minimum of seven days, but depending on your result you may want to wait longer and spend more time reading Chapters 2–6 in this guide and doing the practice tests.

Use the feedback in the notification letter to help you decide which sections in the guide you need to study more carefully.

### What should I do if the level of English was too difficult?

If the level of English was too difficult, look at the English language assessment in Section 3 of Chapter 1 (pages 7–13) to see if your English is at the right level.

If the assessment is too difficult, you should consider attending combined English language and citizenship classes instead of taking the test again. For more information, check Figure 1.1 in Chapter 1 (page 7).

# Practice tests

## Introduction

These practice tests are written in the same format as the *Life in the UK* test. Each practice test has 24 multiple-choice questions. Try timing yourself and see if you can complete a test within the 45 minutes that you will be allowed when you take the official test.

If you get 18 questions or more correct, you have done really well – you are ready to take the *Life in the UK* test.

If you get between 14 and 17 questions correct, you have done well but you need to spend a bit more time reading the study material and completing the *Helping you learn* tasks. You might also want to check the study tips in Section 5 of Chapter 1 for more help (pages 15–21).

If your mark is 13 or less, you need to spend more time reading the study material and answering the *Helping you learn* and revision questions before trying the practice tests again. If your test date is quite soon you may want to reconsider whether you are ready to take it.

# Practice Test 1  ☐ ☐ ☐ ☐ ☐ ☐ ☐

**Question 1.** In the 1950s, where did textile and engineering firms send agents to find workers?

**Answer** (tick one box only)

A. ☐ Australia and South Africa

B. ☐ India and Pakistan

C. ☐ Spain and Portugal

D. ☐ Jamaica and Barbados

---

**Question 2.** Is the statement below TRUE or FALSE?

**Answer** (tick one box only)

True ☐
False ☐
Recently people have come to Britain to find safety, jobs and a better life.

---

**Question 3.** From which TWO of these countries did Jewish people come to Britain to escape racist attacks (pogroms)?

**Answer** (tick two boxes only)

A. ☐ Poland

B. ☐ Germany

C. ☐ Belarus

D. ☐ Lithuania

---

**Question 4.** Which of these statements is correct?

**Answer** (tick one box only)

A. ☐ There are now more women than men at university.

B. ☐ There are now more men than women at university.

**Question 5.**   What percentage of children in Britain today live in lone-parent families?

**Answer**   (tick one box only)

A.   ☐   20%

B.   ☐   25%

C.   ☐   30%

D.   ☐   35%

---

**Question 6.**   In a census, which TWO of the following topics are collected about the population?

**Answer**   (tick two boxes only)

A.   ☐   Occupation

B.   ☐   Height

C.   ☐   Marital status

D.   ☐   Eye colour

---

**Question 7.**   In 2005 the population of the UK was just under:

**Answer**   (tick one box only)

A.   ☐   50 million

B.   ☐   56 million

C.   ☐   62 million

D.   ☐   60 million

---

**Question 8.**   Which of these statements is correct?

**Answer**   (tick one box only)

A.   ☐   Gaelic is spoken in some parts of the Scottish Highlands and Islands.

B.   ☐   Gaelic is spoken in some parts Wales.

**Question 9.** When is Boxing Day?

**Answer** (tick one box only)

A. ☐ The day before Christmas Day

B. ☐ The day after Easter Sunday

C. ☐ The day after Christmas Day

D. ☐ The day before Easter Sunday

---

**Question 10.** Is the statement below TRUE or FALSE?

**Answer** (tick one box only)

True ☐ There are no United Kingdom teams for football and
False ☐ rugby.

---

**Question 11.** Elections in the UK have to be held at least every:

**Answer** (tick one box only)

A. ☐ 4 years

B. ☐ 5 years

C. ☐ 6 years

D. ☐ 3 years

---

**Question 12.** Which of these statements is correct?

**Answer** (tick one box only)

A. ☐ The speaker of the House of Commons is elected by his
or her fellow MPs.

B. ☐ The speaker of the House of Commons is chosen by the
Prime Minister.

**Question 13.**   When was the Parliament of Scotland first formed?

**Answer**   (tick one box only)

A.   ☐   1997

B.   ☐   1998

C.   ☐   1999

D.   ☐   2000

---

**Question 14.**   Is the following statement TRUE or FALSE?

**Answer**   (tick one box only)

**True**   ☐   The UK government has kept the power to suspend the
**False**   ☐   Northern Ireland Assembly.

---

**Question 15.**   Is the statement below TRUE or FALSE?

**Answer**   (tick one box only)

**True**   ☐   When you want to buy a home, you usually do it through
**False**   ☐   an estate agent.

---

**Question 16.**   Which of these statements is correct?

**Answer**   (tick one box only)

A.   ☐   The loan to buy a home is usually paid back over 15 years.

B.   ☐   The loan to buy a home is usually paid back over 25 years.

---

**Question 17.**   People who wish to rent a home can look in:

**Answer**   (tick one box only)

A.   ☐   local newspapers

B.   ☐   libraries

C.   ☐   post offices

D.   ☐   building societies

**Question 18.** Which TWO of the following can help with urgent medical treatment?

**Answer** (tick two boxes only)

A. ☐ GP

B. ☐ Nearest Accident and Emergency department

C. ☐ Local chemist

D. ☐ NHS Direct nurse

---

**Question 19.** Which of these statements is correct?

**Answer** (tick one box only)

A. ☐ You should look for a GP as soon as you move to a new area.

B. ☐ The local hospital will look for a GP for you.

---

**Question 20.** Which TWO of the following are common terms for refuse in the UK?

**Answer** (tick two boxes only)

A. ☐ Waste

B. ☐ Dump

C. ☐ Rubbish

D. ☐ Trash

---

**Question 21.** Which TWO of the following jobs may need a CRB check?

**Answer** (tick two boxes only)

A. ☐ Supermarket supervisor

B. ☐ Childcare worker

C. ☐ Work with vulnerable people

D. ☐ IT engineer

**Question 22.** When you start a new job, your employer should give you a written contract within:

**Answer** (tick one box only)

A. ☐ 2 weeks

B. ☐ 2 months

C. ☐ 10 months

D. ☐ 20 weeks

---

**Question 23.** Which of these statements is correct?

**Answer** (tick one box only)

A. ☐ Sexual harassment can include indecent remarks.

B. ☐ Sexual harassment cannot include comments about the way you look.

---

**Question 24.** Is the statement below TRUE or FALSE?

**Answer** (tick one box only)

True ☐ The law says that, when men and women do the same
False ☐ job, they should receive equal pay.

# Practice Test 2 □ □ □ □ □ □ □ □

| **Question 1.** | By how much is the average hourly pay rate lower for women than men? |
|---|---|
| **Answer** | (tick one box only) |
| A. □ | 10% |
| B. □ | 15% |
| C. □ | 20% |
| D. □ | 25% |

| **Question 2.** | When did women get the right to vote at the age of 21? |
|---|---|
| **Answer** | (tick one box only) |
| A. □ | 1922 |
| B. □ | 1938 |
| C. □ | 1918 |
| D. □ | 1928 |

| **Question 3.** | For which TWO of these reasons do children play outside less today than they did in the past? |
|---|---|
| **Answer** | (tick two boxes only) |
| A. □ | Increased pocket money |
| B. □ | Increased home entertainment |
| C. □ | Increased concern for children's safety |
| D. □ | Increased school hours |

**Question 4.**    Is the statement below TRUE or FALSE?

**Answer**    (tick one box only)

**True**    ☐    Most young people in England take the General
**False**    ☐    Certificate of Secondary Education (GCSE) examinations
at the age of 17.

---

**Question 5.**    Which of these statements is correct?

**Answer**    (tick one box only)

A.    ☐    Current statistics show that about half of the population
have used illegal drugs at one time or another.

B.    ☐    Current statistics show that about a third of the
population have used illegal drugs at one time or
another.

---

**Question 6.**    At what age can young people vote?

**Answer**    (tick one box only)

A.    ☐    17

B.    ☐    18

C.    ☐    19

D.    ☐    21

---

**Question 7.**    Is the statement below TRUE or FALSE?

**Answer**    (tick one box only)

**True**    ☐    Hallowe'en is a day when lovers exchange card and gifts.
**False**    ☐

**Question 8.**   Who is the patron saint of Wales?

**Answer**   (tick one box only)

A.   ☐   St David

B.   ☐   St George

C.   ☐   St Patrick

D.   ☐   St Andrew

---

**Question 9.**   In which city is the Notting Hill Carnival held?

**Answer**   (tick one box only)

A.   ☐   Cardiff

B.   ☐   Edinburgh

C.   ☐   Belfast

D.   ☐   London

---

**Question 10.**   Which TWO of the following are Christian festivals?

**Answer**   (tick two boxes only)

A.   ☐   New Year

B.   ☐   Hallowe'en

C.   ☐   Easter

D.   ☐   Christmas

---

**Question 11.**   What percentage of the UK population attends religious services?

**Answer**   (tick one box only)

A.   ☐   8%

B.   ☐   9%

C.   ☐   10%

D.   ☐   11%

**Question 12.**    What are members of the House of Lords known as?

**Answer**    (tick one box only)

A.    ☐    MEPs

B.    ☐    Cabinet members

C.    ☐    Peers

D.    ☐    GPs

---

**Question 13.**    Is the statement below TRUE or FALSE?

**Answer**    (tick one box only)

**True**    ☐    The British Constitution is written down in a single
**False**    ☐    document.

---

**Question 14.**    How many parliamentary constituencies is the UK divided into?

**Answer**    (tick one box only)

A.    ☐    616

B.    ☐    546

C.    ☐    646

D.    ☐    806

---

**Question 15.**    Which TWO of the following are important agreements produced by the United Nations (UN)?

**Answer**    (tick two boxes only)

A.    ☐    The Convention on the Elimination of All Forms of Discrimination against Women

B.    ☐    The European Convention on Human Rights

C.    ☐    The Children Act

D.    ☐    The Convention on the Rights of the Child

**Question 16.** People who buy their own home usually pay for it with a special loan from a bank. What is the loan called?

**Answer** (tick one box only)

A. ☐ Rent

B. ☐ Mortgage

C. ☐ Statement

D. ☐ Lease

**Question 17.** Which TWO of the following do you dial to call emergency services?

**Answer** (tick two boxes only)

A. ☐ 919

B. ☐ 212

C. ☐ 999

D. ☐ 112

**Question 18.** Which TWO of the following are banknote denominations in the UK?

**Answer** (tick two boxes only)

A. ☐ £10

B. ☐ £25

C. ☐ £50

D. ☐ £100

**Question 19.** Is the statement below TRUE or FALSE?

**Answer** (tick one box only)

**True** ☐ Credit Unions are financial co-operatives.
**False** ☐

**Question 20.** If your child is ill you can ask for information or advice from:

**Answer** (tick one box only)

A. ☐ the ambulance service

B. ☐ the local Health Authority

C. ☐ the local pharmacist

D. ☐ social security

---

**Question 21.** Is the statement below TRUE or FALSE?

**Answer** (tick one box only)

True ☐ Everyone in the UK is allowed to work.
False ☐

---

**Question 22.** Which of these statements is correct?

**Answer** (tick one box only)

A. ☐ Interpreters are available at Jobcentre Plus offices.

B. ☐ Interpreters are not available at Jobcentre Plus offices.

---

**Question 23.** Which TWO of the following are paid for out of the money raised from income tax?

**Answer** (tick two boxes only)

A. ☐ Housing

B. ☐ Roads

C. ☐ Employment agencies

D. ☐ Police

---

**Question 24.** Your CV should include information on:

**Answer** (tick one box only)

A. ☐ your family

B. ☐ your qualifications

C. ☐ your reasons for coming to the UK

D. ☐ your future plans

# Practice Test 3 □ □ □ □ □ □ □

**Question 1.**  Is the statement below TRUE or FALSE?

**Answer**  (tick one box only)

**True**  □  More school-age girls smoke than boys.
**False**  □

---

**Question 2.**  In Britain today what percentage of the workforce is made up of women?

**Answer**  (tick one box only)

A.  □  33%

B.  □  25%

C.  □  45%

D.  □  58%

---

**Question 3.**  Which TWO of the following are common jobs for young people while they are still at school?

**Answer**  (tick two boxes only)

A.  □  Newspaper delivery

B.  □  Delivery driver

C.  □  Work in an office

D.  □  Work in a supermarket

---

**Question 4.**  Between what ages must children attend school in England?

**Answer**  (tick one box only)

A.  □  5 and 16

B.  □  4 and 15

C.  □  5 and 17

D.  □  4 and 16

**Question 5.**  When did a terrible famine occur in Ireland?

**Answer**  (tick one box only)

A. ☐  Mid-1840s

B. ☐  Early 1900s

C. ☐  Early 1820s

D. ☐  Mid-1860s

---

**Question 6.**  When did the First World War end?

**Answer**  (tick one box only)

A. ☐  1914

B. ☐  1920

C. ☐  1918

D. ☐  1939

---

**Question 7.**  In which year will the next census take place?

**Answer**  (tick one box only)

A. ☐  2009

B. ☐  2010

C. ☐  2011

D. ☐  2012

---

**Question 8.**  Which TWO of the following areas of England have large ethnic minority populations?

**Answer**  (tick two boxes only)

A. ☐  The South West

B. ☐  The South East

C. ☐  The North East

D. ☐  The North West

**Question 9.**    In 2005 what percentage of the population lived in Northern Ireland?

**Answer**    (tick one box only)

A.    ☐    3%

B.    ☐    8%

C.    ☐    5%

D.    ☐    6%

---

**Question 10.**    Which of these statements is correct?

**Answer**    (tick one box only)

A.    ☐    5 November is an occasion when people in Great Britain set off fireworks.

B.    ☐    5 November is a day when people play jokes on each other until midday.

---

**Question 11.**    Is the following statement TRUE or FALSE?

**Answer**    (tick one box only)

**True**    ☐    The House of Lords is the more important of the two
**False**    ☐    chambers in Parliament.

---

**Question 12.**    What is the name of the Prime Minister's country house?

**Answer**    (tick one box only)

A.    ☐    10 Downing Street

B.    ☐    Chequers

C.    ☐    Stormont

D.    ☐    Holyrood

**Question 13.** Is the following statement TRUE or FALSE?

**Answer** (tick one box only)

**True** ☐ Only people nominated to represent a political party can
**False** ☐ stand to be elected as an MP.

---

**Question 14.** Which of the following statements is correct?

**Answer** (tick one box only)

**A.** ☐ The government can instruct the police on what to do in
a particular case.

**B.** ☐ The government cannot instruct the police on what to do
in a particular case.

---

**Question 15.** Is the following statement TRUE or FALSE?

**Answer** (tick one box only)

**True** ☐ Half the people in the UK own their own homes.
**False** ☐

---

**Question 16.** Which TWO of the following are organisations that help
the homeless?

**Answer** (tick two boxes only)

**A.** ☐ Shelter

**B.** ☐ Department for Work and Pensions

**C.** ☐ Citizens Advice Bureau

**D.** ☐ Credit union

**Question 17.** Which of these statements is correct?

**Answer** (tick one box only)

A. ☐ A solicitor will provide the legal agreements you need to buy a home.

B. ☐ A bank will provide the legal agreements you need to buy a home.

---

**Question 18.** Is the following statement TRUE or FALSE?

**Answer** (tick one box only)

**True** ☐ There is plenty of council accommodation in the UK.
**False** ☐

---

**Question 19.** Which of these statements is correct?

**Answer** (tick one box only)

A. ☐ If you have a low income or are unemployed you may be able to claim Housing Benefit to help you pay your rent.

B. ☐ If you have a low income or are unemployed you may be able to claim Housing Benefit to help you pay your mortgage.

---

**Question 20.** Which of these statements is correct?

**Answer** (tick one box only)

A. ☐ The minimum wage for people aged 22 or over is £5.35 per hour.

B. ☐ The minimum wage for people aged 22 or over is £6.15 per hour.

**Question 21.** What must your employer give you each time you are paid?

**Answer** (tick one box only)

A. ☐ Pay slip

B. ☐ P45

C. ☐ P60

D. ☐ Contract

---

**Question 22.** Which TWO of the following are refugees entitled to, as soon as their asylum applications are successful?

**Answer** (tick two boxes only)

A. ☐ The right to vote

B. ☐ The right to buy a house

C. ☐ The right to work

D. ☐ The right to a National Insurance number

---

**Question 23.** Which of these statements is correct?

**Answer** (tick one box only)

A. ☐ The main aim of a trade union is to improve the working conditions of its members.

B. ☐ The main aim of a trade union is to promote fair trade internationally.

---

**Question 24.** Is the following statement TRUE or FALSE?

**Answer** (tick one box only)

True ☐ Everyone who lives in the UK is entitled to Jobseeker's
False ☐ Allowance and maternity pay.

# Practice Test 4 □ □ □ □ □ □ □

**Question 1.**    In the 2001 general election how many first-time voters used their vote?

**Answer**    (tick one box only)

A.    ☐    One in three

B.    ☐    One in four

C.    ☐    One in five

D.    ☐    One in six

---

**Question 2.**    Is the statement below TRUE or FALSE?

**Answer**    (tick one box only)

**True**    ☐    Until 1887 a married woman had no right to divorce her
**False**    ☐    husband.

---

**Question 3.**    How many young people go on to higher education at college or university?

**Answer**    (tick one box only)

A.    ☐    One in four

B.    ☐    One in three

C.    ☐    One in five

D.    ☐    One in six

**Question 4.**   Why did the Huguenots come to Britain in the 16th and 18th centuries?

**Answer**   (tick one box only)

A.   ☐   To trade with Britain

B.   ☐   To invade Britain

C.   ☐   To escape religious persecution

D.   ☐   To find work

---

**Question 5.**   In the late 19th and early 20th centuries why did the Suffragettes demonstrate?

**Answer**   (tick one box only)

A.   ☐   For the right to divorce their husband

B.   ☐   For the right to go out to work

C.   ☐   For the right to vote

D.   ☐   For the right to move home

---

**Question 6.**   Is the following statement TRUE or FALSE?

**Answer**   (tick one box only)

**True**   ☐   Women over the age of 30 were given the right to vote
**False**   ☐   when the First World War ended in 1918.

---

**Question 7.**   What percentage of all ethnic minority people live in London?

**Answer**   (tick one box only)

A.   ☐   45%

B.   ☐   40%

C.   ☐   35%

D.   ☐   42%

**Question 8.**   Is the statement below TRUE or FALSE?

**Answer**   (tick one box only)

**True**   ☐   There are more people over 60 than children under 16 in
**False**  ☐   the UK.

---

**Question 9.**   Where is John O'Groats?

**Answer**   (tick one box only)

**A.**   ☐   The south-west corner of England

**B.**   ☐   The north-west of England

**C.**   ☐   The north coast of Scotland

**D.**   ☐   The east coast of Scotland

---

**Question 10.**   Who is the head, or Supreme Governor of the Church of
England?

**Answer**   (tick one box only)

**A.**   ☐   The Prime Minister

**B.**   ☐   The Archbishop of Canterbury

**C.**   ☐   The Queen

**D.**   ☐   The Chancellor of the Exchequer

---

**Question 11.**   The Cockney dialect is spoken in which city?

**Answer**   (tick one box only)

**A.**   ☐   Liverpool

**B.**   ☐   London

**C.**   ☐   Manchester

**D.**   ☐   Sheffield

**Question 12.** Who are civil servants?

**Answer** (tick one box only)

A. ☐ Government ministers

B. ☐ Members of the Opposition

C. ☐ Managers and administrators who carry out government policy

D. ☐ Pressure and lobby groups that try to influence government policy

---

**Question 13.** Is the following statement TRUE or FALSE?

**Answer** (tick one box only)

True ☐ The UK was a member of the European Union (EU) when
False ☐ it formed in 1957.

---

**Question 14.** What is the aim of the Commonwealth?

**Answer** (tick one box only)

A. ☐ For member states to function as a single market

B. ☐ To draw up conventions and charters that focus on human rights

C. ☐ To promote the use of the euro

D. ☐ To promote democracy and good government and to eradicate poverty

---

**Question 15.** Council tax applies to which TWO of the following types of property?

**Answer** (tick two boxes only)

A. ☐ Bungalows

B. ☐ Offices

C. ☐ Houseboats

D. ☐ Shops

**Question 16.** How many Assembly Members are there in the National Assembly for Wales?

**Answer** (tick one box only)

A. ☐ 65

B. ☐ 60

C. ☐ 55

D. ☐ 50

**Question 17.** Which of the following is the Home Secretary responsible for?

**Answer** (tick one box only)

A. ☐ Law

B. ☐ Health

C. ☐ Education

D. ☐ Agriculture

**Question 18.** Which of these statements is correct?

**Answer** (tick one box only)

A. ☐ Electricity in the UK is supplied at 240 volts.

B. ☐ Electricity in the UK is supplied at 220 volts.

**Question 19.** Which TWO of the following are terms for accommodation you can rent from the local authority?

**Answer** (tick two boxes only)

A. ☐ Social housing

B. ☐ Council housing

C. ☐ Local housing

D. ☐ Benefit housing

**Question 20.** Is the following statement TRUE or FALSE?

**Answer** (tick one box only)

**True** ☐ Water is supplied free to all homes in the UK.
**False** ☐

---

**Question 21.** A landlord usually asks for a deposit to cover:

**Answer** (tick one box only)

A. ☐ any damage

B. ☐ electricity and gas bills

C. ☐ maintenance of the property

D. ☐ rates

---

**Question 22.** Is the statement below TRUE or FALSE?

**Answer** (tick one box only)

**True** ☐ An employment contract will show the hours to be
**False** ☐ worked.

---

**Question 23.** Which TWO of the following can you speak to if you are
worried about health and safety at work?

**Answer** (tick two boxes only)

A. ☐ Police

B. ☐ Supervisor

C. ☐ Trade union representative

D. ☐ Newspaper

---

**Question 24.** If you lose your job you may be entitled to:

**Answer** (tick one box only)

A. ☐ maternity pay

B. ☐ compensation

C. ☐ redundancy pay

D. ☐ retirement pay

# Answers to practice tests

## Practice Test 1

| Question | Answer |
| --- | --- |
| 1. | B |
| 2. | True |
| 3. | A and C |
| 4. | A |
| 5. | B |
| 6. | A and C |
| 7. | D |
| 8. | A |
| 9. | C |
| 10. | True |
| 11. | B |
| 12. | A |
| 13. | C |
| 14. | True |
| 15. | True |
| 16. | B |
| 17. | A |
| 18. | A and B |
| 19. | A |
| 20. | A and C |
| 21. | B and C |
| 22. | B |
| 23. | A |
| 24. | True |

# Practice Test 2

| Question | Answer |
| --- | --- |
| 1. | C |
| 2. | D |
| 3. | B and C |
| 4. | False – most young people take GCSEs at 16 |
| 5. | B |
| 6. | B |
| 7. | False – young people often dress up in costumes and play 'trick or treat' |
| 8. | A |
| 9. | D |
| 10. | C and D |
| 11. | C |
| 12. | C |
| 13. | False – the British Constitution isn't written down |
| 14. | C |
| 15. | A and D |
| 16. | B |
| 17. | C and D |
| 18. | A and C |
| 19. | True |
| 20. | C |
| 21. | False – some people need work permits |
| 22. | A |
| 23. | B and D |
| 24. | B |

# Practice Test 3

| Question | Answer |
| --- | --- |
| 1. | True |
| 2. | C |
| 3. | A and D |
| 4. | A |
| 5. | A |
| 6. | C |
| 7. | C |
| 8. | B and D |
| 9. | A |
| 10. | A |
| 11. | False – the House of Commons is the more important chamber in Parliament |
| 12. | B |
| 13. | False – anyone can stand to be elected as an MP |
| 14. | B |
| 15. | False – two-thirds of people in the UK own their own homes |
| 16. | A and C |
| 17. | A |
| 18. | False – there is a shortage of council accommodation in the UK |
| 19. | A |
| 20. | A |
| 21. | A |
| 22. | C and D |
| 23. | A |
| 24. | False – only those who pay enough NI contributions are entitled to Jobseeker's Allowance and maternity pay |

# Practice Test 4

| Question | Answer |
|----------|--------|
| 1. | C |
| 2. | False – it was in 1857 that married women first had the right to divorce their husbands |
| 3. | B |
| 4. | C |
| 5. | C |
| 6. | True |
| 7. | A |
| 8. | True |
| 9. | C |
| 10. | C |
| 11. | B |
| 12. | C |
| 13. | False – the UK joined the European Union (EU) in 1973 |
| 14. | D |
| 15. | A and C |
| 16. | B |
| 17. | A |
| 18. | A |
| 19. | A and B |
| 20. | False – water rates are charged to supply water to homes |
| 21. | A |
| 22. | True |
| 23. | B and C |
| 24. | C |

# Answers to revision questions

## Answers to revision questions for Chapter 2

1. To find safety, jobs and a better life
2. New laws were introduced restricting immigration to Britain
3. Because there was a shortage of labour in the UK
4. 1928
5. Suffragettes
6. Women
7. 65%
8. Increased home entertainment
   Increased concern about child safety (although there is no evidence that this danger is increasing)
9. Ages 5 to 16
10. Vocational qualifications
    General Certificates of Education at Advanced Level (AGCEs) in England (also known as A Levels)
    Higher/Advanced Higher Grades in Scotland
11. One in three
12. 14
13. 18
14. 18

## Answers to revision questions for Chapter 3

1. No
2. Scotland
3. 14 February
4. 2011
5. London
6. Horse race
7. 31 December
8. 84%
9. Archbishop of Canterbury
10. 10%

## Answers to revision questions for Chapter 4

1.    Prime Minister
2.    No – the speaker is neutral
3.    No
4.    No
5.    No
6.    Yes
7.    A non-departmental government body
8.    Member of the European Parliament
9.    27
10.    1999
11.    No – the House of Lords isn't democratically elected
12.    Yes
13.    No – the UK has a free press

## Answers to revision questions for Chapter 5

1.    Two-thirds
2.    It depends on the size and value of your property
3.    Your local authority, Citizens Advice Bureau and Mediation UK
4.    12
5.    60 mph
6.    Three years
7.    18
8.    Yes
9.    No
10.    People's Dispensary for Sick Animals (PDSA)
11.    16
12.    Local authority
13.    Education Maintenance Allowance
14.    Yes

## Answers to revision questions for Chapter 6

1.    The National Academic Recognition Information Centre – it provides guidance on overseas qualifications
2.    12

3. £5.35
4. HM Revenue and Customs
5. 13
6. A Criminal Records Bureau check
7. Curriculum vitae
8. It provides useful work experience
   It helps you get involved in your local community
9. Two months
10. Jobseeker's Allowance

# Resources, references and useful websites

## Books

**Home Office (2007) Life in the United Kingdom: A Journey to Citizenship**. Published by The Stationery Office (TSO), London, and available from TSO. You can buy the book from many bookshops or from the online bookshop at **www.tsoshop.co.uk**.
The book is available in the following formats:

Paperback (2nd edition, 2007)
ISBN 978 0113413133  £9.99

Large print version (2nd edition, 2007)
ISBN 9780113413171  £9.99

Downloadable pdf (2nd edition, 2007)
ISBN 9780113413232  £9.99 (£11.49 inc. VAT)

Audio CD (2nd edition, 2007)
ISBN 9780113413188  £9.99 (£11.49 inc. VAT)

**NIACE (2007) ESOL and citizenship: A teachers' guide**, by Chris Taylor.

**Home Office (2008) Life in the United Kingdom: Official citizenship test study guide**. Published by The Stationery Office (TSO), London.

**The Stationery Office (2009) Passing the Life in the UK Test: Official Practice Questions Book**. Published by The Stationery Office (TSO), London.

## Useful websites and phone numbers

*Life in the UK* test website: **www.lifeintheuktest.gov.uk**

Helpline    08000 154245
This provides useful information about the test, including finding your nearest test centre and help with using a computer keyboard and mouse.

Directgov – the official government website for citizens:
**www.direct.gov.uk**
The website provides easy access to the public services and information about them.

United Kingdom Parliament website: **www.parliament.uk**
The official website for the UK Parliament, providing information about the House of Commons and the House of Lords.

Office for National Statistics website: **www.statistics.gov.uk**
This website provides a vast amount of statistical information about the UK, including the economy, the census, population and employment.

Devolved administration websites:

| | |
|---|---|
| Wales | **www.wales.gov.uk** |
| Scotland | **www.scottish.parliament.uk** |
| Northern Ireland | **www.niassembly.gov.uk** |

| | |
|---|---|
| Commonwealth website: | **www.thecommonwealth.org** |

Provides information about the work of the Commonwealth and the 53 member states.

| | |
|---|---|
| Border Agency website: | **www.bia.homeoffice.gov.uk** |
| Immigration Enquiry Bureau | 0870 606 7766 |
| Nationality Contact Centre | 0845 010 5200 |

This website has information about British citizenship, studying and working in the UK and how the UK borders are managed.

Citizens Advice websites: **www.citizensadvice.org.uk** and
**www.adviceguide.org.uk**
An online Citizens Advice service that provides independent advice on your rights, including benefits, housing, employment rights and discrimination, debt and tax issues.

NHS websites: **www.nhs.uk** and **www.nhsdirect.nhs.uk**
Provide advice and guidance on health matters and using NHS services.

| | |
|---|---|
| Learndirect website: | **www.learndirect.co.uk** |
| Learndirect | 0800 101 901 |

Provides online courses in basic English and Maths as well as a range of courses in IT and Business and Management. You can also use the website to find a local Learndirect centre.

# Notes